The CHICAGO ENTREPRENEUR'S SOURCEBOOK

Your Complete Guide to ■ Starting Smart, ■ Finding Resources for Growth & ■ Creating Your Survival Network

MELISSA GIOVAGNOLI

JOAN-MARIE MOSS

Enterprise · Dearborn
a division of Dearborn Publishing Group, Inc.

While a great deal of care has been taken to provide accurate and current information, the ideas, suggestions, general principles and conclusions presented in this text are subject to local, state and federal laws and regulations, court cases and any revisions of same. The reader is thus urged to consult legal counsel regarding any points of law—this publication should not be used as a substitute for competent legal advice.

Publisher: Kathleen A. Welton
Acquisitions Editor: Patrick J. Hogan
Associate Editor: Karen A. Christensen
Interior Design: Professional Resources & Communications, Inc.
Cover Design: Westdal Design

Published by Enterprise • Dearborn
A division of Dearborn Publishing Group, Inc.

Printed in the United States of America

92 93 94 10 9 8 7 6 5 4 3 2 1

Library of Congress Cataloging-in-Publication Data

Giovagnoli, Melissa
    The Chicago entrepreneur's sourcebook: your complete guide to starting smart, finding resources for growth & creating your survival network / Melissa Giovagnoli, Joan-Marie Moss.
      p. cm.
    Includes bibliographical references and index.
    ISBN 0-79310-479-3
    1. Industrial management—United States—Information services—Handbooks, manuals, etc. 2. Business information services—United States—Handbooks, manuals, etc. 3. New business enterprises—Illinois—Chicago—Information services—Handbooks, manuals, etc. 4. Business enterprises—Illinois—Chicago—Information services—Handbooks, Manuals, etc.   I. Moss, Joan-Marie.   II. Title.
HD30.36.U5G56 1993   92-6637
016.6581'1'0977311—dc20   CIP

ADVANCE PRAISE FOR *THE CHICAGO ENTREPRENEUR'S SOURCEBOOK*

"Whether you are struggling to stay afloat, just beginning, or even doing well with your enterprise, this gold mine will enrich your future."

Og Mandino
Author, *The Greatest Salesman in the World*

"In the Chicagoland area there is no shortage of resources. The trick is knowing where to go to find them and how to access them. When seeking assistance for your small business, go to *The Chicago Entrepreneur's Sourcebook*."

Sam McGrier
Small Business Administration

"Whether your business is an idea, acorn-sized, or mature and expanding like a giant oak, *The Chicago Entrepreneur's Sourcebook* will make your growth easier."

Roberta Janis
Loop Small Business Development Center

"*The Chicago Entrepreneur's Sourcebook* is the small business owner's scout . . . providing direction, access and information about Chicago's best kept secrets."

Mollie Cole
Illinois Department of Commerce and Community Affairs

"Many enter the world of entrepreneurship without sufficient planning or preparation. When trouble comes, they have no idea of the vast network of resources and advice available. This resource may save such a business."

Holly Trueblood
Chicagoland Enterprise Center

■ Dedication ■

To Pat and Traci Moss, Marianne and Jay Cochrane, Joseph VandenHeuvel and Judy and Al Pioch.
—Joan-Marie Moss

To my grandmother, Posselina Haims, my husband, Steve, and my father, Al Goodman.
—Melissa Giovagnoli

■ Acknowledgments ■

We wish to acknowledge the Illinois Department of Commerce and Community Affairs (DCCA) for the resource information it provided us. We applaud the efforts of our state to address the needs of its growing small business community. We thank the Small Business Administration (SBA)—particularly Sam McGrier and Steve Konklin, who contributed information on Illinois SBA programs. We would also like to thank Tom Kleve, a commercial banking analyst from Household International. Finally, we salute the many people in the small business community from whom we have learned—our instructors, our mentors, our competitors and our colleagues.

■ Contents ■

Chapter 8 Marketing Your Business 111

Chapter 9 Government and Educational Resources 135

Chapter 10 Networking 156

■ Preface ■

The Chicago Entrepreneur's Sourcebook is the result of our interaction with hundreds of entrepreneurs who have struggled with trying to find information on how to start and grow their businesses successfully. These professionals have shared their frustrations and their insights, and we consider them contributors to this book.

Although by no means exhaustive, this book attempts to address the most common concerns of small businesses throughout the Chicagoland area. We found that when you know what to look for, there is no end to the amount of assistance available to entrepreneurs. Today, more than ever, small business is considered a viable, valuable market segment; and, new resources are constantly being created to support its development.

It is projected that the number of new small businesses entering the market throughout the 1990s will be staggering, creating as many as 30 percent more jobs. That increase, however, should not be surprising. It's a natural response to current economic conditions, including: downsizing of major corporations; loss of jobs in both blue-collar and white-collar levels; and the trend toward integration of family and personal goals with career goals. Between 1980 and 1990, Fortune 500 companies eliminated 3.4 million jobs. Companies with fewer than 500 employees *created* 13 million jobs.

Both of us have found that an entrepreneurial approach works well despite the challenge of balancing home and business demands. We have discovered that this lifestyle is far superior to clocking in at someone else's office. We have also found that, despite times of economic struggle, functioning as a small business does, in fact, work. It puts food on the table while giving us a sense of satisfaction not experienced elsewhere.

As a small business owner, you will work much longer and harder than you ever did for any employer. Your drive, stick-to-it-iveness, energy and talents will be tested as never before. But the rewards are enormous. We will be among the first to stress that small business is not for everyone. If you attempt to go into business for the wrong reasons and without adequate preparation, you may be doomed to failure before you even start. For this reason, we urge you to think through the process carefully and research your business ideas thoroughly before making the big change.

You must go into business with both eyes open and with a single-minded approach if you hope to succeed. The pitfalls are many. Only those who are prepared and recognize those pitfalls will succeed.

We have compiled this information and list of contacts to help you achieve your maximum potential. Take advantage of the information to create your own opportunities.

We can't do the work for you, but we have attempted to create a road map to clearly mark the way. Be patient. You will need to ask many questions and do countless hours of homework. You will still need to doggedly pursue the answers you need. But this book should help you save many hours.

■ Introduction ■

How To Use This Book

The mission of *The Chicago Entrepreneur's Sourcebook* is to provide an accessible, easy-to-use guide containing the resources that we have uncovered during our 15 plus years of doing business as entrepreneurs and many more years of counseling others.

We have used the following format to highlight resources within the chapters :

■ Resource _____

Name of Resource:	This section provides you with the name of the resource. If it is a book, it will be a title. If it is an organization, it will be the name and address of the organization. If it is a general resource, it will be a resource heading. Check the Index for help in locating information.
Where To Find It:	Sometimes the resource will be available in your local library. If the resource is an organization, we list addresses and telephone numbers.
Who Could Use It:	Often the resource is useful for any entrepreneur. However, there are some cases when the resource was created for a specific group of entrepreneurs—women, manufacturers, etc.
What It Contains:	This section provides you with an overview of what information is available from the resource.

Why Use It:	This section shows you what type of benefit you can derive by using the resource.
When To Use It:	This section addresses the best time to use the resource.

_____ ∎

Note: These headings are used as guidelines. Whenever a heading is unnecessary, due to redundancy or obvious focus, it has been eliminated.

The *Sourcebook* is organized into chapters that address the major needs of both start-up and established entrepreneurs. The questions entrepreneurs ask most frequently involve money and financing. Chapter 5, "Assessing Start-Up Needs," will help you determine costs. Chapter 7, "Financing Resources," suggests where to go for financing. You will need a business plan, and you will find information about creating one in Chapter 6.

Use the Table of Contents to zero in on the areas where you need help. The *Sourcebook* should be your reference on where to find help for whatever business question you are facing. Our overriding message is to be informed, so please pay special attention to Chapter 4, "Business Information Research," which provides direction on how to use the library to get information for your business.

The resources in this book are usually very inexpensive and, we feel, useful as well. Please note, however, that we cannot guarantee the effectiveness of any resource. While we or our colleagues have personally used many of the resources, this does not apply to all. We have attempted to be comprehensive. It is up to you to decide whether a particular resource is helpful, given your circumstances.

A Word of Advice

Keep an open mind when contacting resources. You will have better results if you are patient and make *resourcing*, as we call it, part of your long-term plan. Realize that the person who might be helping you is just one person in an organization. If you don't get the results you were looking for, ask for someone else. Take advantage of the information boom. Never before have there been so many resources available for your benefit.

As you read this book, we hope that you will discover many useful resources for building a successful business. Throughout our research and writing, we have been surprised by the deluge of information that is constantly being developed for the entrepreneur. At the pace we are now receiving new information, it is likely that by the time you finish reading this book there will be dozens of new magazines, classes, associations and support systems.

Therefore, we ask that you accept the challenge of staying informed. We hope to update this book regularly and invite you to take an active role in that process. If you find that you have used or are currently using a resource that is particularly beneficial to your business, please take the time to let us know. Share your resources with others.

We have included a form for you to indicate resources you have found most helpful. If we use a resource you recommend, we will credit you in our next edition.

■ One ■

Profile of the Entrepreneur

■

Altogether the successful small business owner is intelligent and possesses an inquisitive, innovative, and creative mind. He can perceive and process information quickly and accurately, and has the energy and flexibility needed to handle most contingencies. He also has the initiative, drive, forcefulness, and impatience to make things happen. And he has the ability to listen and the desire to make everyone happy and to treat them with dignity and respect.

"Portrait of a Successful Small Business Owner," from *Small Business Reports*, January 1990

The Small Business Administration defines small business in terms of sales or number of employees: any wholesale business with annual sales below $7.5 million; any retail business with annual sales under $1.5 million; a construction business with less than $3 million in annual sales; or a manufacturing business with less than 250 employees. The state of Illinois recognizes a business as *small* when it is comprised of less than 50 employees, does

1

less than $4 million in annual sales and is not dominant in its field.

But small business actually defies definition. Often the term refers to people—frequently working from home—who sell services and products that are the result of their own talents and resources. Their efforts are generally categorized as *lifestyle* businesses, and owners of such businesses frequently have difficulty. The annual income of such business owners is much lower than you might expect—around $25,000. Their companies might generate much higher revenues, but their personal compensation, after paying for operating expenses, is typically low. Like much larger businesses, they must abide by tax regulations, zoning laws and other limitations.

Whether you operate a "lifestyle" business or a much larger small business, you belong to what is now recognized as the fastest-growing segment of today's economy. Because of this rapid growth, *entrepreneur* and *small business owner* have become the buzzwords of the decade. Although these terms are used interchangeably in this book, a clarification is in order. Not all small businesses are entrepreneurial. Entrepreneurs strive to realize their fullest potential, working on their own terms while maintaining control of the administrative end of the business. Relying on their flexibility and ability to make quick strategic decisions, they focus on identifying and capitalizing on opportunities that arise out of shifts in the market. Typically they maintain a proactive business style, rather than simply reacting to outside pressures. Entrepreneurs take on the risks of decision-making and accept responsibility for the successes or failures that result from their decisions.

Risk and the Entrepreneur

Entrepreneurs are known to be risk takers—but they aren't reckless. Some of the techniques they use to minimize their risks include:

- *Asking the right questions, starting with: "What if. . .?" and "If I take this risk, what is the worst that can happen?"* Preplanning and groundwork are essential to taking calculated risks— they help entrepreneurs address the issues and skirt worst-case scenarios.

- *Researching the market, constantly asking questions* Entrepreneurs realize that customers, competitors and suppliers hold the keys to their success.
- *Evaluating choices by identifying the range of outcomes from worst-case to best-case scenarios* Entrepreneurs may use a schematic number line from -5 to +5, the Ben Franklin close, listing pros and cons for each choice, case histories, *gut* feelings or some other method of comparison and evaluation to keep them on track.
- *Looking beyond costs and examining how easy or difficult a start-up would be* What are user perceptions, timing and other crucial factors? Entrepreneurs realize that numbers aren't the whole picture.
- *Evaluating all risks in terms of overall goals and objectives*

Since many entrepreneurs start their businesses with personal savings and function on the financial edge, risk-taking skills are critical. Even those who start with solid financial backing will be confronted with risks—and calculated risks can offer the opportunity to grow and move forward. Whether starting a new business or growing an existing one, an entrepreneur needs to be armed with every available resource in order to overcome the challenges ahead.

How To Be Successful

Our motto is, "Why reinvent the wheel?" Let it be yours. Start-up entrepreneurs often mistakenly believe that in order to succeed they must have a product or service that is far superior to their competition. What is really needed is a competitive advantage. It only takes a small improvement on what the competition is doing to create a successful business.

For the most part, businesses grow in stages. Finding good resources will bring about growth opportunities for your company. Persistence will be your ally. Continuous learning and resource gathering are important keys to your success. You will need to be assertive. Entrepreneurs are doers. They rarely say, "It can't be done." Instead, they say, "Let's find a way to do it."

If you want to be a successful entrepreneur, you must proceed with your eyes wide open. We recommend that you:

- *Review your business.*   What could you do to be different—to stand out among all your competition, to improve your work, to instill a sense of excitement in your business? Look ahead. Read product and trade papers. Study market trends and keep looking ahead.
- *Ask successful people the secret of their success.*   Invite them to lunch or coffee. Truly successful people share. Their insights and experience are invaluable resources that can save countless hours of misdirected efforts.
- *Advance your education and follow-up on available resources every chance you get.*   Libraries, workshops, seminars, colleges, community colleges and publications are irreplaceable support mechanisms for the small business owner.
- *Get rid of your deadweight, wasted time and nonproductive products or services.*   Introduce new products or services that speak to the needs of the market.
- *Follow your hunches.*   If you have taken the time to obtain adequate information, these hunches will be solidly grounded and trustworthy.
- *Don't pin your hopes on luck.*   Be ready. Prepare in advance. Join the team. Get into the game.

The Entrepreneurial Climate of the 1990s

The 1990s strategy involves coping with change. Four areas affect the way entrepreneurs will do business today and tomorrow:

- Rising international markets and the movement toward sponsorship of business by government in foreign countries
- Keener competition in an unpredictable environment
- Turbulence in the marketplace
- The element of surprise that pervades the business climate

You must be able to sense when your environment is changing. Don't assume that the marketplace is there. You have to research, develop and build your marketplace.

Flexibility and resiliency are more important now than ever before. Learn by doing, and profit from customer feedback. Be a market-driven business adapting and changing to meet the demands of the market. Remember, most products are incremental improvements—not originals. Look at this as an asset. A small, flexible company can change and achieve more than a big corporation because it can adapt to changes more quickly.

Begin by taking a good hard look at the market in which you will be functioning. Have a clear understanding of how your business can fit into the larger picture. To do this, learn to read the signs that are all around us:

- The market is in the midst of a tremendous shift.
- Companies in special market segments are experiencing phenomenal growth. They are centered in the areas of recreation, health and child care, marketing, recreation, technologies of all sorts and businesses that cater to an aging market.
- At the same time, large companies are laying off thousands of workers—both blue-collar and white-collar. "Mean and lean" is the economic buzzphrase of the year—perhaps of the decade.

Because there are no guarantees in today's work force, many of the more skilled individuals (who have the most difficulty securing new employment) are already looking for alternatives. Thousands of new businesses have been started in recent months, and thousands more will be started in years to come. Self-employment is a particularly attractive option for those who have come to realize that the only real stability is that which they create for themselves.

This idea is not new. Until the rise of industrialism in the mid-nineteenth century, the United States economy was based on individual enterprise. At that point, the focus of business shifted to mass production and market control. No longer was individual enterprise considered worthy. Growth and control of the marketplace gave rise to the corporations—the Fortune 500—that we know today. Entire populations moved to the large cities. By the middle of the 20th century, the successful were recognized primarily by their climb up the corporate ladder rather than by significant individual achievements.

We are experiencing a swing of the pendulum. We've reached and passed the peak of the trend toward industrialization and, many experts say, are simply returning to a more balanced economy. The deregulation of Ma Bell and the downsizing of other monoliths heralded the coming of a new era. Over the past few years, thousands have lost positions with large corporations that were once considered invincible. At first the losses were in blue-collar areas. But, by 1992 successful white-collar employees found that they, too, were expendable.

The employees left in *mean and lean* downsized companies still must produce. Downsizing has left enormous holes in the economy where the small businesses can fill a need. Since those still employed are limited by time and resources, they must increasingly rely on outside vendors for services and products that had traditionally been produced in-house.

While the thought of creating a small business may seem a very attractive alternative, a word of caution is in order—there are many pitfalls. Get in the wrong business (one that fails to satisfy a real need in this newly emerging market), take wild risks that you aren't ready for, fail to do your homework, ignore the market indicators, and you can fall flat on your face.

There is a wealth of information and assistance out there. The federal government, the state government and the marketplace are encouraging us to look at small business as a viable alternative. Special training programs, counseling, tax breaks, financial assistance and educational opportunities are increasing. But no one is going to search them out for you, and no one is going to make it easy. It's going to be a struggle and, as always, those who survive and prosper will be those who use available resources wisely.

Until recently, new businesses needed to ferret out resources as best they could. They often discovered that resources were few and far between. They also found a tremendous resistance to their vision of success as individual entities in competition with the market giants. Even today we find pockets where small businesses have credibility problems. And frequently, it was difficult for newly created businesses to establish their credibility without vast infusions of monies to sustain them.

But this is changing rapidly. Today, it isn't nearly as difficult to establish a business account with banks and suppliers as it was 50 or even 10 years ago. And in many municipalities there are no longer restrictions on working out of one's home.

Of course, there is a lot more work to do. There is still no single definition—acceptable across the board—for what really constitutes a small business. For example, real estate brokers, artists, writers and others still find themselves disqualified from programs and financing slated for the small business. Frequently, independent proprietors in the business of providing services are told that they really don't have a business because their receipts aren't substantial.

Overview of the Chicago Business Market

Small and medium-sized businesses have contributed the majority of jobs for Americans in recent years. Small Business Administration (SBA) data indicate that more than 43.7 percent of the 113 million employed American workers are employed by smaller businesses—companies with fewer than 100 employees.

Today, small business means big business. Small businesses currently represent more than 98 percent of all United States companies. They employ more than half of the private work force and produce almost 50 percent of the Gross National Product. Nearly two out of every three new jobs are the results of small business growth.

Contrary to what many believe, it is small businesses— in fact, very small entrepreneurial businesses—that have provided our country with the majority of new jobs during the past decade. More than 88 percent of all business establishments are owned by small businesses. While small businesses with fewer than 100 employees created almost all of the employment growth, the number of jobs created by big business barely increased at all.

Chicago is also the home of many women-owned businesses. The $9.2 billion generated by its 89,424 women-owned firms in 1987 resulted in the *City That Works* being ranked third in the nation in terms of women-owned firms.

Overall, the state of Illinois has seen an increase in business start-ups over the past five years. According to a recent article in *Crain's Chicago Business*, 29,000 businesses—sole proprietorships, partnerships and corporations—made Illinois their home last year. Cook County alone receives more than 500 sole proprietorship and partnership dba (doing business as) filings monthly.

What types of businesses are being developed? More than 90 percent of all start-ups have been in the service sector. A good portion of these start-ups have been business services: accounting, consulting, high-tech, health and engineering. Cook County is home to the nation's fifth largest concentration of electronics companies and ranks third largest in corporate research and development. Additionally, Chicago is third in the nation for its number of health care facilities. There has also been significant growth in software, telecommunications and pharmaceutical companies. The remaining start-ups have been predominantly in the area of light manufacturing.

Focusing on the majority—the service sector—it is clear that these companies have less initial financial risk and lower start-up capital requirements, but they face increasing difficulty when it comes to expansion. It is their lack of assets in the form of equipment and inventory that often prevents them from obtaining loans for expansion. This problem is becoming more and more of a concern as many of the companies that started in the past decade are stagnating from an inability to secure growth capital. Chicago banks are just beginning to address this need through partnerships with the Small Business Administration (SBA) and the state.

With a recession that some believe will last at least another year, government, educational institutions and even large corporations are beginning to focus on small business. Support is increasing slowly. Efforts are being made to reach out to smaller businesses to help them become more competitive in our emerging global marketplace. One such effort is being made by the Department of Commerce and Community Affairs (DCCA), the business arm of the state government that has undergone extensive restructuring to create new small business development centers that will better address the needs of small businesses.

Entrepreneurial Survival Skills

Regardless of the economy's climate, many entrepreneurs survive and prosper. Common traits of the survivors include:

- They are always ethical, even when times are hard.
- They know their customers' needs and satisfy them.

- They take the time to do something extra for their customers.
- They focus their energies on the bottom line rather than on growth for growth's sake.
- They pay special attention to accounts receivable.
- They control their inventories, keeping them close to sales.
- They reduce expenses.
- They know how to minimize paperwork.

Survival also requires caution against the pitfalls of operating a small business. Below are the most common causes of small business failure.

- *Inadequate capital*   Be prepared with hard cash for months—even years—of sustained losses. Always prepare for the worst-case scenario.
- *Inexperienced management*   Get some sound experience in managing *before* you go into business, or seek the advice of a good management consultant as you grow your business.
- *Failing to detect bad credit risks early*   Develop the ability to read the warning signs: collection claims, suits and judgments (get credit reports on your larger customers); reluctance to provide audited financial statements and bank references; partial/erratic payments on account; unusually large orders.
- *Mistaking a hobby for a business*   Hobbies can be the basis for promising business ventures if creative or technical skills required for the hobby are balanced with strong business sense and know-how.
- *Trying to make the business appeal to everyone*   Remember less is more. Focus on a single age category, a single socioeconomic group, a single selling point. Narrow your focus, identify a specific market segment, and utilize every available resource to become a significant factor in that area.
- *Underpricing the product/service*   The right price should balance the company's need to make a profit and the consumer's search for value. Establish the range you feel meets both needs, research your market and build intangibles (prestige, status, pride).

Types of Small Businesses

Small businesses can take a wide variety of forms, including:

- *Freelancing*   writers, designers, photographers, etc.
- *Part-Time Opportunities*   in almost every type of business
- *Consulting Practices*   management, marketing, computer opportunities and more
- *Professional Practices*   doctors, lawyers, accountants, other licensed individuals
- *Manufacturing Representatives*   to represent large companies and their products from your home
- *Franchises*   hundreds become available yearly, some with very low start-up fees
- *Service Businesses*   from business services such as telecommunications, computer repair and maintenance, commercial real estate and leasing, to consumer services like diaper services, home health care and personal shoppers
- *Manufacturing*   combining importing and exporting opportunities with a good product
- *Retail Stores*   filling a need in a niche market

Most professions require that you have formal training and licensing prior to opening your business practice. However, most other business categories require much less in the way of formal schooling. No matter what business you're in, you must have a solid skill base. Too many entrepreneurs put their time and money into businesses that require more expertise than they currently have. For example, a person with little or no background in computers might start a business selling computers. If you find you need more skill development, consider taking a part-time job in your area of interest.

Some businesses are risky even if you have the right experience. It would be unwise, for example, for a couple to quit their jobs, and put all their current savings into a restaurant. According to many business consultants, including the financial lending division of the SBA, restaurants are high risks, so risky, in fact that many banks and the government won't loan on such ventures.

Whatever you do, when choosing a business, make it one that you are sure you will enjoy. While you're waiting for the dollars to roll in, you will need a business that satisfies more than just your financial needs.

What about You?

Where do you fit in? If you're looking for the magic guaranteed-to-succeed, can't-fail road to riches, security and notoriety, forget it. There is no BEST business, but you can select one that is best for you:

- *Know yourself, your talents, what you enjoy and don't enjoy doing.* Are you creative or more comfortable accomplishing tasks that are predictable and repetitive? If you need help identifying your interests and talents, seek help from career counselors (available through many colleges at very low fees) or personal development specialists.
- *Research until you find an idea (maybe even one that is working for someone else).* Improve it, change it, mold it to fit you and your strengths, and look for ways to make it most profitable for you.
- *Organize yourself.* If you don't take the time to get organized now, you will never catch up.
- *Take a chance.* Step out of your comfort zone. Allow yourself to take small risks in order to achieve the possibility of growth and profits.
- *Learn how to live with less for a while.* Work smarter, applying your mind, your energy and your spirit rather than throwing money at problems.
- *Get help.* Consult professionals and experts in your industry.
- *Set clear goals and bottom lines for yourself and your business.* A solid business plan is essential.

From Idea to Planning

If you are still questioning what type of business to start, or whether to start one at all, call the Illinois Business Hotline, (800) 252-2923, and order the *One-Stop Business Start-Up Kit*, which is described in detail in the next chapter. The kit's Feasibility Checklist contains a series of questions designed to help you evaluate the financial success of your proposed business concept. Use it *before* investing extensive time or money in a business.

As you read through the next chapters, take time to investigate the many resources available to you prior to start-up. Keep a large notebook with divisions for marketing, management, financial and legal information. Schedule weekly sessions to review the material you have collected, either on your own or with another business friend or small business counselor. Constantly summarize the information you have gathered, and incorporate anything relevant in your business plan.

Most start-ups take six to eight weeks, if not longer, before they open their doors for business. Remember, a little planning can go a long way. Once you begin operating, you have almost no time for planning. Enjoy this time; don't be overly anxious. It's important to start on firm ground. When you're in business and several months have gone by (and you will be amazed how quickly they do), you will have trouble remembering a time when you weren't working ten hour days. The time spent in the planning stage is crucial to the success of your business.

■ **Two** ■

Start-Up
Requirements

■

Starting a business can often be confusing. Not only are there local ordinances to follow, but state and federal regulations as well. Luckily, the government offers a simple way to obtain most of the forms for start-up. This information is listed below along with a breakdown of other considerations.

While this chapter provides an overview of start-up requirements, it is not meant to replace professional advice. We encourage you to seek counsel from an accountant and/or an attorney as soon as possible. Help is also available from any of the state's small business development centers (see Chapter 9, "Government and Educational Resources"). It is very important that you consider the type of business you plan to open, and select a legal structure that will be most beneficial to your potential growth. The extra time taken at start-up will be well worth it later—as your business grows, so does your potential legal exposure.

Checklist for Start-Up

Following is a list of considerations you should address before opening the doors of your new business:

Check Local Zoning Laws, Municipal Ordinances and Deed Restrictions

Some areas restrict home-based business occupations. Call your town or county clerk (at your village hall) to obtain information on possible restrictions in your area and to determine whether you need a license to run your business out of your home. Also, if it applies to your circumstances, check with your homeowners association or examine your house deed for restrictions.

Choose a Legal Name

All individuals who will be operating a business under names different than their personal names are required to file an Assumed Name Act Registration Form (to be filed with the County Clerk in the county where you will run your business), often called a *dba* (doing business as). These businesses are also required to publish in a newspaper of general circulation, located within the county, notification of the assumed name once a week for three consecutive weeks.

Check with the county clerk or secretary of state to see if the name you've chosen has been taken already.

Set Up a Legal Form of Business

Prior to start-up it is important to determine the legal structure of your business.

Common Legal Structures

Some common legal start-up structures are summarized below. You are encouraged to seek additional advice from an attorney and/or an accountant.

Sole Proprietorship

One individual maintains complete control and responsibility for the business. Business losses and gains are personal losses and gains and filed on a Schedule C Tax Return.

Advantages	Disadvantages
Ease of formation	Less access to capital and financial resources

Relative freedom from government controls	Less protection with regard to personal liability (You as an individual are separate from your corporate entity.)
Less costly accounting fees	

Partnership

The business is owned and operated by two or more people who are co-owners. Before starting a company under this legal structure, it is highly recommended that a written agreement be drawn up by an attorney creating the partnership and specifically covering all contingencies. The partnership agreement should define the ownership percentages of each partner, limits of responsibility and work requirements, as well as when and how the partnership might be dissolved. The partnership is responsible for filing tax returns with each partner reporting his or her own share of the earnings on his or her individual 1040 tax return.

Partnerships enable you to focus on personal strengths while relying on your partner's strengths. When partnering with an established firm, such an arrangement can provide more predictability of demand for your product/services.

Advantages	**Disadvantages**
Easier to form than the corporation	As with a sole proprietorship, general (versus limited) partners are personally liable.
Sharing expenses of start-up partnership	

Limited partners are exposed only to the extent of their investment in the partnership.

Limited Partnership

Under the Illinois Revised Uniform Limited Partnership Act of 1986, limited partnership filings become centralized with the Secretary of State. Filing requirements are substantially different. Contact an attorney regarding this filing. For additional information, contact the Secretary of State:

Limited Partnership Division
Centennial Building, Room 330
Springfield, IL 62756
(217) 785-8960

Corporation

A corporation is a legal entity that is more complex than either the sole proprietorship or the partnership. In this structure, you are required to file incorporation papers that create an entity that continues to perpetuity. This structure relieves you of some liability, allows you to raise expansion capital more easily and is heavily regulated. Costs of incorporation range from $450 to $1,000. Income is taxed first as earnings to the firm and then again as personal income when owners receive dividends, salaries, etc. Best when you have employees, a corporation protects liability.

A corporation may sell shares of stock and certificates of ownership to fund the start-up and the growth of the corporation. The shareholders then elect a board of directors. The board elects a president of the company and other officers who run the company on a day-to-day basis. The company is then responsible for paying taxes on revenues.

An alternative to this formation is the *Subchapter S Corporation* (*S Corporation*) where the losses or gains of the company flow through the corporation and are paid as a personal loss or gain. To qualify for S Corporation status, a corporation must meet several requirements, one of which limits the number of shareholders to 35. Additionally, all shareholders must consent to the corporation choice of S Corporation status. For further information on forming an S Corporation, call the Internal Revenue Service at (800) 424-3676.

Advantages	Disadvantages
Limited personal liability	More costly for start-up and yearly taxes
Relatively easy to transfer ownership	

Note: The corporation is the most complex form of business, and it is wise to do a great deal of research prior to making a decision in favor of this business form. Check the United States Small Business Administration (SBA) pamphlet, *Incorporating a Small Business*, prepared by the Office of the General Counsel. And confer with both an attorney and an accountant to determine how requirements will affect your methods of operation.

Publications

How To Form Your Own Corporation Without a Lawyer for Under $75, Ted Nicholas. Dearborn Financial Publishing, 1992.

Incorporating a Small Business, prepared by the Office of the General Counsel, United States SBA Management Assistance, Support Services, Management Aid Number 6.003 A free publication. Write to PO Box 15434, Fort Worth, TX 76119.

"Selecting the Legal Structure for Your Business," SBA Directory of Business Development Publications. This form is in the *One Stop Business Start-up Kit*, available free from the Illinois Business Hotline, (800) 252-2923. It identifies the various legal structures that a small business can use in setting up operations, listing the advantages and disadvantages of each.

State and Local Requirements

The majority of laws you must follow upon start-up are mandated by the state. Because laws and regulations are subject to constant change, it is important that you seek the counsel of an attorney who specializes in corporate law.

In Illinois the following state agencies are working for you:

Small Business Assistance Bureau

A department within DCCA that has created a *Small Business Development Center Network* in cooperation with the SBA, colleges and universities and private business organizations. The network of centers throughout the state includes:

- *Small Business Development Centers*
- *Procurement Assistance Centers*
- *Technology Commercialization Centers*
- *Small Business Incubators*

Services provided by these centers and incubators include: assistance with fulfilling state requirements, preparing business and marketing plans, securing capital, improving business skills, accessing international trade opportunities and addressing other business management needs. There are also programs specifically targeted to assist minority and women-owned businesses.

Where To Find a Center   See Chapter 9, "Government and Educational Resources," or call the Illinois Business Hotline.

The Illinois Business Hotline (800) 252-2923

The state has developed a special hotline to help make starting-up much easier. Use the hotline to obtain business plans, details about registration, licensing requirements, SBA publications, counseling assistance and general start-up information. We will refer to the hotline frequently throughout this book.

The One-Stop Business Start-Up Kit

Obtain the applications for licenses, registrations, permits and tax forms required for your business free of charge. The *Start-Up Kit* includes:

- *Checklist for Going into Business*   This Feasibility Checklist is available through the SBA Directory of Business Development Publications.
- *A Business Plan*   Choose from: "The Business Plan for Home-Based Business," "Business Plan for Retailers," "Business Plan for Small Construction Firms," "Business Plan for Small Manufacturers," "Business Plan for Service Businesses."
- *Assumed Name Act Registration Form*   File with the clerk in the county where you will run your business. All businesses are required to register with the local clerk when they operate under any business name other than the full legal name of the persons owning and operating the business are required to file this form, often called a dba (doing business as). These businesses are also required to publish notification of the assumed name once a week for three consecutive weeks in a newspaper of general circulation located within the county.
- *Application for Employer Identification Number (SS-4)*   Every partnership, corporation and S Corporation must have a Federal Employer Identification Number (FEIN) to use as its taxpayer identification number.
- *Business Registration Kit*   This part includes:Illinois Business Taxpayer Application for Registration (NUC-1)
- *Notice of Sale/Purchase of Business Assets (Form NUC-542-A)*   Complete this form if you have bought your business from someone. If you do not complete the form, you may have to

pay any taxes, penalties and interest owed to the Illinois Department of Revenue by the former owner.

- *Retailer's Tax Booklet (ST-19)*   If you are planning to resell items, you may be required to pay sales tax.
- *Income and Replacement Tax Accounts Information*
- *Illinois Income Tax Act Withholding Tax Guide and Tables (IL-700)*   If you pay wages to yourself or any employees, you are required to pay taxes on those wages.
- *Withholding Exemption Certificate (IL-W-4)*
- *Withholding Tax Payment Form (IL-501)*
- *Quarterly Withholding Tax Return (IL-941)*
- *Business Classification Codes Information*
- *Request for Income Tax Forms Sheet*

Note: If you need additional assistance to complete any of these forms, call the Illinois Department of Revenue at (800) 732-8866 between 8:00 A.M. and 5:00 P.M., Monday through Friday.

- *Articles of Incorporation*   If you are planning to incorporate, you are required to file Articles of Incorporation (BCA-2.10) with the Secretary of State that will, among other things, indicate the purpose of your business. Additional information on incorporating is available from the offices of the Secretary of State, Business Services:

Centennial Building, 3rd Fl.
Springfield, IL 62756
(217) 782-6961

17 N. State St., Ste. 1137
Chicago, IL 60601
(312) 793-3380

Licenses for Special Occupations

In Illinois, many businesses are required to be registered and/or licensed by the Department of Professional Regulation.

■ Resource

Name of Resource:	Department of Professional Regulation
Where To Find It:	320 W. Washington St., 3rd Fl. Springfield, IL 62786 (217) 785-0800 or Call the Department of Professional Regulation at the Illinois Business Hotline—(800) 252-2923
Who Could Use It:	The following occupations/career areas are licensed or registered by this department:

Alarm Contractor
Architect
Athletic Trainer
Barber
Beautician
Chiropractor
Collection Agency
Controlled Substance Dealer
Cosmetologist
Dentist
Detection of Deception Examiner
Funeral Director
Embalmer
Esthetician
Land Sales
Land Developer
Land Surveyor
Licensed Practical Nurse
Nurse
Nursing Home Administrator
Occupational Therapist

Optometrist
Pharmacist
Physical Therapist
Physician
Physician Assistant
Podiatrist
Professional Boxer/Wrestler
Professional Engineer
Professional Service Corp.
Psychiatrist
Psychologist
Real Estate Broker
Real Estate Salesperson
Real Estate Time-Share
Roofing Contractor
Shorthand Reporter
Social Worker
Structural Engineer
Surgeon
Veterinarian

What It Contains: Information on licensing
Why Use It: Required by state law
When To Use It: Prior to start-up

Taxes

If you have employees or decide to pay yourself wages, certain taxes must be taken from these wages and paid to the government. They include:

Withholding Taxes
Federal Income Taxes
State Income Taxes
FICA (Social Security)
Unemployment Insurance

Federal Income Taxes

You may be required to register with both the federal government and the state of Illinois for withholding purposes. Additionally, you may be required to withhold taxes if you are paying wages to yourself or to an employee. For information about federal taxes, call the Department of Revenue Hotline at (800) 732-8866, and ask for the *Federal Tax Kit* for a sole proprietorship, partnership or corporation. Additionally, you can ask that *A Tax Guide for Small Business* (Publication 334) and *Employer's Tax Guide* (Publication 15) be sent to you. We recommend that you seek advice from an accountant regarding wages.

■ Resource

Name of Resource:	Internal Revenue Service Taxpayer Hotline
Where To Find It:	Taxpayer Information and Education Branch Taxpayer Service Division 1111 Constitution Ave., N.W. Washington, DC 20274 (800) 829-1040
What It Contains:	The hotline is the place to go for answers to questions such as: How much can you deduct for business meals? How much can you deduct for a home-based business? How much can you deduct for travel expenses? You can also order a Federal Employer Identification Number (FEIN), an updated *Small Business Tax Guide* or a *Start-Up Kit*.

State Income Taxes

To register with the state of Illinois, call the Department of Revenue Hotline at (800) 732-8866, or contact the Department of Revenue at:

100 W. Randolph, Concourse 300
Chicago, IL 60601
(312) 814-5258
or
101 W. Jefferson St.
Springfield, IL 62794
(217) 785-3707

Unemployment Insurance

You may be required to pay unemployment insurance contributions if you have:

- employed one or more workers in each of 20 or more calendar weeks, or
- paid at least $1,500 in total wages during the quarter.

Contributions are due no later than the last day of the month following the calendar quarter in which liability was incurred.

Note: You may also be required to pay this insurance if you buy a business that is already subject to the terms above.

Contact: Department of Employment Security
401 S. State St.
Chicago, IL 60605
(312) 793-4880

Start by requesting the *Report To Determine Liability Form* included in the *One Stop Business Start-Up Kit* that can be obtained by calling the Illinois Business Hotline, (800) 252-2923.

When To Use It   This form should be used prior to start-up, or once you begin paying wages that equal 3.4 percent (current rate) of an employee's yearly gross salary up to $9,000. The contribution may be made in a lump sum, but employee salary payments must still be reported for each quarter.

Note: There are varying rates for certain businesses such as construction, manufacturing, mining and transportation. Contact the Department of Employment Security at the number listed above to receive more detailed information.

Federal Employer Identification Number (FEIN)

Partnerships, corporations and S corporations are required to have an FEIN number. Sole proprietors should also consider securing an FEIN even though they can use their social security numbers. There is an important advantage to obtaining an FEIN number—it can help you keep personal income separate from business income.

■ Resource _____

Name of Resource: IRS Hotline (to obtain a form)
Where To Find It: (800) 829-1040
or *One Stop Business Start-Up Kit*
(800) 252-2923 (form is included in the kit)

| **Why Use It:** | Required for all but sole proprietorships |
| **When To Use It:** | Prior to start-up |

■

Note: Some sole proprietors may be required to obtain an FEIN, if they: pay wages to one or more employees, or file any excise tax returns, including those for alcohol, tobacco or firearms.

All other sole proprietors may use their social security numbers as their business taxpayer identification numbers.

Insurance and Personnel Requirements

It is imperative that you seek professional counsel regarding state and federal mandates governing your personnel policies:

■ Resources

	Either through a private insurance agent or contact:
Name of Resource:	Illinois Industrial Commission
Where To Find It:	100 W. Randolph, 8th Fl.
	Chicago, IL 60601
	(312) 814-6611
Who Could Use It:	Any business with employees. Temporary workers are provided workers' compensation even though they do not receive any other company benefits.
What It Contains:	Insurance for accidental death or injuries to employees; insurance premiums are based on total company payroll, loss experience and type of business.
Why Use It:	Under the Workers' Compensation and Workers' Occupational Diseases Acts, an employer is required to provide insurance for accidental deaths or injuries and occupational diseases of employees arising in the course of employment. The insurance requirement is applicable to all businesses and must include provisions for all medical expenses, rehabilitation and retraining, temporary and total disability, permanent disability and death benefits.

Name of Resource: Personnel Posting Requirements
Where To Find It: For Wage and Hour Poster:
                          U.S. Department of Labor
                          Wage Hour Division
                          230 S. Dearborn, Rm. 412
                          Chicago, IL 60604
                          (312) 353-8145
                          For Occupational Safety and Health
                          Administration Poster:
                          U.S. Department of Labor
                          OSHA
                          230 S. Dearborn, Rm. 3244
                          (312) 353-2220
                          For Age Discrimination/Equal Employment
                          Administration Poster:
                          Equal Employment Opportunity Commission
                          Control Division
                          536 S. Clark, Rm. 988
                          Chicago, IL 60605
                          (312) 353-8985
Who Could Use It: Any business with employees
What It Contains: Posters
Why Use It: It is required by law that certain posters be
                          displayed on business premises to inform
                          employees of their rights and benefits.
When To Use It: When you have one or more employees

━━━━━━━━━━━━━━━━━━━━━━━━━━ ■

Copyrights, Trademarks and Patents

Be aware that you cannot copyright your facts or ideas, but you can copyright the written form of your presentation. If you have multiple pieces of material on one subject, you can group them together. Brochures, training materials, articles, etc. are examples of copyright-eligible materials. For further information, call the U. S. Copyright Office, (202) 479-0700.

Information & Publications Section, LM-455
Library of Congress
1st and Independence Ave. SE
Washington, DC 20540

(800) 347-1997—Federal Information Center (to obtain forms)
(202) 707-3000—Copyright Office (to talk to an information specialist)
(202) 707-9100—Information Hotline (for general information and to order publications)

To register your work with the Copyright Office:

- Request a copyright application from the Copyright Office.
- Within three months of publication, send the completed application form and two copies of your work, along with a $20 registration fee, to the Copyright Office.

Additionally, for your own protection, we strongly recommend the following:

- *Disclosure Letter*   At the inception of your project, write a letter describing your idea, detail your research and work done to date, cite the people contacted in your research. Date, notarize and file your letter.
- *Log/Journal*   You must have an active business and verify ongoing work. To be legal, this must be a bound book with consecutively numbered pages, written in ink with *no* erasures. (Corrections are to be lined through.) Include names of all the people you met with, the times of the meetings, dates and locations pertinent to the project.

Check with the Patent and Trademark Office or an attorney. First you must use the TM regularly in the course of business, and then file an application for trademark with the Patent and Trademark Office in your state and/or at the federal level. Call the Federal Information Center (800) 347-1997 for details. Information is also available from the Commissioner of Patents and Trademarks (703) 308-4357 or the Chicago Public Library (312) 747-4300.

Trademarks (TM) and Servicemarks (SM) are registered in the state of Illinois by filing application with:

Office of the Secretary of State
Index Division
111 E. Monroe
Springfield, IL 62756
(217) 782-7017

To find an attorney who specializes in copyright and trademark law, call the Illinois State Bar Association Lawyer Referral Service at (800) 252-8916. Residents of Cook County may contact the State Bar Association's Chicago Referral Service at (312) 554-2001.

■ Resources

Name of Resource:	Lawyers for the Creative Arts
Where To Find It:	213 W. Institute Pl., Ste. 411 Chicago, IL 60610 (312) 944-ARTS
What It Contains:	A staff of volunteer lawyers and consultants are available to answer questions on copyrights and refer you to lawyers who specialize in copyright laws.
Why Use It:	To access information and resources and sources of assistance in copyright issues
Name of Resource:	Inventor's Council
Where To Find It:	53 W. Jackson, Ste. 1643 Chicago, IL 60604 (312) 939-3329
Who Could Use It:	Anyone who is either planning to invent or has already invented a product
What It Contains:	The council provides assistance to inventors in such areas as patent issues and product commercialization, holds monthly meetings and sponsors free workshops and seminars.
Why Use It:	If you have invented a product
When To Use It:	Prior to introducing product
Name of Resource:	Science and Technology Information Center (STIC)
Where To Find It:	The Chicago Public Library Business/Science/Technology Division 400 S. State St. Chicago, IL 60610 (312) 269-2865
Who Could Use It:	Any business producing a new product

What It Contains: STIC has a patents collection that includes complete runs of U.S. patents since 1871, as well as a complete run of British patents since 1617. There are U.S. Patent Office indexes and publications to facilitate patent searches.

Note: The *Trademark Register of the United States* can be consulted to find out if a specific trademark has already been registered. STIC is also useful for locating technical information on manufacturing processes.

Why Use It: To discover if a particular product has already been created. It is also useful to check with the Center to find out if another business has a similar or the same name.

Publications

Fishman, Stephen, *The Copyright Handbook, How To Protect and Use Written Works*. Nolo Press, 1992.

Nicholas, Ted, *How To Get Your Own Trademark*. Dearborn Financial Publishing, Inc., 1993.

Booklets Available from SBA. (Order forms are available in the *One Stop Business Start-Up Kit*. Call:(800) 252-2923)

   Can You Make Money with Your Idea or Invention?   This is a step-by-step guide that shows how you can make money by turning your creative ideas into marketable products. It is a resource for entrepreneurs attempting to establish themselves in the marketplace.

   Introduction to Patents.   This booklet offers some basic facts about patents to help clarify your rights. Additionally, it discusses the relationships among business, an inventor and the Patent and Trademark Office to ensure protection of your product and to avoid or win infringement suits.

■ Three ■

Building Your Team of Experts

■

Entrepreneurs need others to help them grow successfully, and that includes seeking the advice of a lawyer and an accountant. Most entrepreneurs also rely on outside specialists to balance their areas of weakness. Keep this adage in mind: "Do what you do best and hire out the rest."

This chapter offers a variety of resources directed at growing your team of business experts—from accountants and attorneys to telecommunications and entrepreneurial specialists.

Legal Resources

It is important that you seek legal advice prior to start-up. Choose an attorney who specializes in corporate law. Don't be afraid to ask for a preliminary interview—many attorneys offer a free first-time consultation. Talk to two or more attorneys to get an idea of how the profession works, and ask for references from each. Bring written questions. Ask about their billing practices.

When To Seek Legal Counsel

You should contact an attorney for the following reasons:

- To discuss the type of business organization that best suits your needs
- To learn the local, state and federal regulations that will affect your business
- To obtain licenses and permits
- To have contracts prepared or inspected
- If you will be creating contracts with suppliers or customers
- If you will be leasing space—to handle lease agreement negotiations/inspections
- If you will need insurance coverage, or in anticipation of negotiations with employees or partners
- If you will be creating employment contracts

■ Resources _____

Name of Resource:	Illinois State Bar Association
	Legal Referral Service
Where To Find It:	(800) 252-8916
What It Contains:	Referrals for attorneys in specialty fields
Why Use It:	As a resource for finding good legal counsel
Name of Resource:	*Martindale-Hubbel Law Directory*
Where To Find It:	Local library—reference section
Who Could Use It:	Any business
What It Contains:	Listings and ratings of attorneys—listed by city and state
Why Use It:	To find attorneys with a corporate law specialization who are conveniently located near your business
When To Use It:	Prior to start-up or as needed

Publications

Hancock, William A. *Small Business Legal Advisor*. McGraw-Hill, 1992. Provides legal advice for the small business. Use this book to get a good overview of the legal requirements for start-up.

Steingold, Fred S. *The Legal Guide for Starting and Running a Small Business.* Nolo Press, 1992.

Accounting Resources

Prior to start-up, it is also wise to talk to an accountant. Ask your attorney or banker to provide a referral. Your business will require the following accounting services:

Auditing   Financial statements certified by a CPA are often requested from banks or other lenders when a loan is pending.

Bookkeeping   Either an accountant or an independent bookkeeper can help you set up an accurate recording of your company's cash receipts, disbursements, sales and operating expenses. This person can also help you prepare periodically: a statement of assets and liabilities as of a given date (balance sheet), a statement of operating results for a given period of time (income statement), a statement of changes in financial position.

Note: It is often recommended that smaller businesses use a bookkeeper for monthly record maintenance. Bookkeeping specialists charge lower fees than accountants and are extremely capable.

Taxes   Tax services provided by accountants include: planning transactions for the lowest present and future tax liabilities; preparing tax returns; conferring with tax authorities who are examining prior years' tax returns; and estate planning.

Consulting   Because of their experience with many companies in many industries, accountants may be able to help you reduce your costs, improve reports, install or upgrade accounting systems (manual and automated), budget and forecast, while handling financial analysis, production control, quality control, personnel compensation and records management.

The resources listed below can be helpful when you are looking for accounting assistance.

■ Resource _____

Name of Resource:	Illinois CPA Society/Foundation
Where To Find It:	222 S. Riverside Plaza, 16th Fl.

What It Contains: Chicago, IL 60606
(312) 993-0393 or (800) 572-9850
Assistance in securing an accountant ∎

Banking Resources

Commercial Checking Accounts

Checking account services usually include custom check design and a variety of check formats that provide audit controls for your account. Service charges vary among banks, so it is smart to call several banks to see what they charge. The charges are usually calculated on the number of checks written and the number of deposits made, plus a monthly maintenance fee.

Commercial Deposit Services

Commercial bulk deposits allow you to process bulk change, pick up currency or drop off large deposits. (Don't forget 24-hour automatic teller machines. They allow you greater access to several banking services.)

Federal Tax Depository Services also are available to help prevent a penalty for late payment of taxes. The date the bank accepts the deposit establishes the date of payment.

Commercial Savings/Investment Services

Some banks offer corporate savings accounts. Ask about this when you open your checking account. Business Savings Programs allow a business to deposit up to a certain amount in a savings account that earns interest on a percentage per year, compounded continuously for an effective yield. Short-term investments also are available using Certificates of Deposit and Repurchase Agreements.

Insurance Resources and Consultants

Many start-ups don't think about insurance, but it is extremely important. Adequate insurance can protect you from losses even if you operate from home. Ask about a Business Owners Plan (BOP). Get prices for fire, liability, vehicle and workers' compensation coverage. Other types of insurance coverage include: business interruption, crime and key employee.

A good insurance program begins with someone you can trust. Talk with several insurance agents. Ask them to analyze your risks, and study the cost of covering those risks. Your local chamber of commerce is a good place to ask about locating insurance agents. Also, consider using the Better Business Bureau to check someone you are considering hiring. Find someone who will continually reevaluate your risks as you grow. Look for someone who has good relationships with 15 or more of the top financially rated insurance companies.

There are basically three types of insurance agents to choose from. They are:

- *Independent Agents*   Independent contractors, usually representing one or two insurance companies, who issue policies binding their companies directly
- *Brokers*   Professionals who represent a buyer of insurance rather than a company (Unlike independent contractors, brokers cannot bind insurance coverage immediately. They negotiate with underwriters to obtain insurance.)
- *Direct Writers*   Salaried employees or exclusive agents of an insurance company

A fourth type of insurance specialist, rather new to the field, is the independent consultant. Rather than selling insurance, this person works as a consultant to you, providing advice on coverage, pricing, carrier solvency and service quality of a number of insurance companies. These consultants are paid on a fee basis. This type of consulting has grown in the last few years due to the ever increasing complexities of the insurance industry. Many smaller companies hire such consultants to keep their insurance costs down. Recent surveys have shown that insurance costs are a major concern facing small businesses today. Paul Kinsley, an independent consultant located in the Chicagoland area, comments, "Choosing any insurance specialist has to start with trust. You may come across people that call themselves independent consultants, but they aren't if they also sell insurance. If you choose to look for an independent, find someone who works on a fee basis."

Fees start at about $50 per hour. Depending upon the amount and type of insurance you buy, independent consultants can save you a substantial amount of money.

Insure Your Business

Cover inventory, your health, liability for injuries or damages. You may need a homeowner's policy rider if you work out of your home. Insure equipment and your office separately. Do not include office insurance under a homeowner's policy unless you use a *home office rider* or addendum. Look for a replacement cost policy. You may also need an umbrella liability policy to cover things like customers getting hurt on your property. In Chapter 11 we recommend several pamphlets that explain insurance options, such as *Business Life Insurance* prepared by the Institute of Life Insurance and *Insurance Checklist for Small Business* by Mark R. Greene.

Entrepreneurial Consultants

Literally hundreds of consultancies with a variety of specialties reside in Chicago. Rather than attempting to list all of them here, we refer you to Tom Camden and Susan Schwartz's book *How To Get a Job in Chicago*. Updated yearly, this is a wonderful addition to your resource library. In addition to listing Chicago's 1,500 major employers, it contains listings of management consultants as well as information on selected Chicago area professional organizations, networks, clubs and societies.

If you are looking for specialists—in computer, engineering, environmental or marketing, check with trade associations, chambers of commerce or among your professional associates. Also, try:

Dun's Consultants Directory
Dun and Bradstreet Information Services
(800) 526-0651

Check the *Crain's Chicago Business* special yearly supplement that lists the top consultants in the city in various specialties. A partial listing of entrepreneurial consultants is listed below.

■ Resources _____

Name of Resource: Elan Associates
Where To Find It: 79 W. Monroe, Ste. 1320
                          Chicago, IL 60603
                          (312) 782-6496
What It Contains: Provides services for new business start-up, marketing and name selection; organization development and evaluation; and introduction and effective use of microcomputers.

Name of Resource: Irving Graff Business Consultant
Where To Find It: 8655 N. Olcott Ave.
                          Niles, IL 60714
                          (708) 965-1101
What It Contains: Provides consulting services to industry and nonprofit organizations with an emphasis on long-term and short-term business planning. Assists in the start-up stage and offers seminars in this area. Uses more than 30 proprietary software packages to solve various business problems.

Name of Resource: George S. May International Co.
Where To Find It: 303 S. Northwest Hwy.
                          Park Ridge, IL 60068
                          (708) 825-8806
What It Contains: General management consultants concentrating on the problems of small-sized and medium-sized companies. Offers programs in organization, profit and expense control, cash flow and finance, inventory, production control and sales planning. Runs a productivity council for small-sized to medium-sized businesses. Offers "Business Track," a computerized business performance tracking system, designed for smaller businesses.

Name of Resource: Hal Wright
                          The Wright Track

Where To Find It:	PO Box 2416
	Oak Park, IL 60303
	(708) 771-5146
Who Could Use It:	Any established small business that might benefit from a professional consultation
What It Contains:	Works closely with selected businesses, mostly home-based sole proprietors, that demonstrate determination and potential.

Telecommunications Consultants

Pat David, a sales and telecommunications specialist in Chicago, offers the following overview of telecommunications for the small business owner.

"The telecommunications (telephone, computer, etc.) requirements of your new or expanding business—often overlooked as strategic elements of doing business—warrant preliminary planning. Without careful consideration of the nature and the frequency of telephone conversations, problems may result."

Imagine that all your marketing efforts have been fruitful and that your product or service is in demand, but your telephone system cannot accommodate the volume of calls (in or out) that you are experiencing.

Spending a small amount of time with an independent telecommunications consultant before making telecommunications related decisions can provide you with valuable insight to the right types of equipment and services for your business. The time and money invested with an independent consultant is typically a fraction of the time you might waste with a host of vendors who are only interested in selling **their** products to you. The proper application of telecommunications technology can help streamline your business operations and ensure that your customers can reach your business.

Sales and Marketing Consultants

Many entrepreneurs choose to start their own businesses because they have a proven skill in a specific area or an idea for a product that they believe others will be willing to buy. Unfortunately, many businesses don't succeed because of the failure to communicate the values of a product or service to the buying public.

A sales consultant can help you gain the most return from your marketing dollars by helping you to develop a methodology for selling to your target market, communicating your product's unique values, creating concise proposals and more importantly, developing effective closing skills.

Whether you are the salesperson in your organization, or you hire someone to perform this important function, the sales process implemented should be one that is customized to your product or service. Otherwise, you may run the risk of learning too late that the same practices that sold another product or service will not necessarily sell yours.

■ Four ■

Business Information Research

■

Major corporations spend millions of dollars on research. Entrepreneurs hoping to compete in the marketplace can learn from their example. Research is one of the best strategies businesses of all sizes can use to effectively claim a share of the market. The hours of research invested in building a quality resource base inevitably result in a significant savings of both time and money.

As more and more businesses open up, competition is growing across all markets. Unfortunately, very few smaller businesses take the time to research or plan. Instead, they often jump into a market they expect to be profitable. At first, they might actually be successful. However, getting new customers is one thing; keeping them is an entirely different story.

An overwhelming number of consumers report that they have been the recipient of mailings that have no importance to them—which means a lot of money is being wasted. It is important to remember that the age of mass marketing is over, replaced by the current trend toward targeted marketing. Every year better research tools are introduced to help smaller businesses target a special niche market—too small for many larger competitors but large enough to provide a solid business opportunity with growth potential. Using these tools to research the market, the competition and potential customers can tell you very quickly *what* you should be selling to *whom*.

This chapter shows you how to build a resource base through the use of secondary sources. An explanation of each form of research is provided. By taking the time to build a business resource base of your own, you will soon discover the magic of information gathering.

Primary Research

Primary research involves gathering information firsthand—by going to the source itself. You can do primary research almost anywhere at any time. All you need to do is locate people who have information about your industry that you don't currently have. Constantly be on the lookout for opportunities to learn more about your industry, your market, the economy, demographics, trends and effective strategies. Such knowledge will help you identify potential customers as well as competitors. Primary research includes:

- *Observing* Watch how others buy from your competitors. This form of research is particularly useful if you are involved in a retail business; you can go directly to your competitors' stores and watch how they interact with customers. Observing can help you find better ways of delivering your product or service.
- *Talking* Whether you decide to conduct informal research such as random, in person or phone interviews, or more formal research, which is often done in paid focus groups, talking to potential buyers of your product or service is very valuable. You can learn what people are currently thinking. You can research today and implement tomorrow.
- *Shopping* By comparison shopping you can find out what your competition is offering and at what price. Although some entrepreneurs aren't comfortable with calling their

competition to ask what they are charging, others use this form of research as an effective way of pricing their products or services.

Secondary Research

Secondary research involves information gathered indirectly from a third source. Publications such as books and magazines, are the best examples of secondary resources. Much of the information you will gather regarding your target market will be in the form of secondary research. Michael Lavin, in his book *Business Information*, emphasizes that there are advantages and disadvantages to secondary research. He comments that it is "the most difficult to manage, least utilized, but most cost-effective information category."

One of the best places to look for secondary research is your local library. There you can find a wealth of useful business information to help you:

- Locate new customers or clients.
- Target new market segments.
- Identify new products or services.
- Obtain information on competitors.
- Develop written marketing and sales materials for your business.
- Define where your advertising should be directed and determine whether your messages are effective.
- Identify spending habits within your market area and any shifts in those habits.
- Indicate where and how to be most easily accessible to your customers (i.e., location, times).

Using the Library

Your best friend in the search for business information will be the reference librarian at your local library. Librarians have a wealth of resources at their fingertips, and are trained to use them efficiently. Look for a public library or nearby college or university that has a strong business section.

Take full advantage of the interlibrary loan system, which makes a wide variety of books available to even the smallest library. By using interlibrary loan, you will have access to many of the resources referred to in this book.

Tips for Making Your Library Search Easy

To locate resources in a reference book, check the index. Begin by scanning the headings to get a general idea of how topics have been grouped. Since different terms are often used for similar topics, a brief look can help you locate something you may not have found by looking under only one heading.

Use more than one reference book. Check as many references as possible to compile a comprehensive list of resources. Many researchers make the mistake of looking at only one or two information sources. However, no two reference books are exactly alike. Material is compiled differently (through telephone surveys, questionnaires, etc.) or contains diverse information. By checking at least three reference books, your conclusions will be more reliable.

Beware of outdated material! Libraries purchase materials as often as their budgets allow. Directories that are two, three or more years old may be outdated. In fact, even current directories, depending upon the subjects they cover, can be out-of-date. Take the time to make preliminary calls to your targeted resources to update your information.

Many libraries now have access to a database research network—an electronic source of information accessible via computer modem. Ask about it. The amount of material you will receive as the result of such a search will more than compensate you for any charges levied. This database is particularly efficient because it is staffed by highly trained research experts. Some libraries even offer searches, up to a certain dollar limit, free of charge to cardholders. Call your library for more information.

Ask for assistance. If one library does not have the reference book you are looking for, ask the reference librarian if he or she can locate a library where it is available. Take the time to get the references you need. A short trip to another library or utilization of interlibrary loan will be worth it.

Take regular trips to the library. Try to spend at least one day a month visiting the reference section of your library. Ask the reference librarian if any new resources or updates have come out. Take a quick walk through the reference section. Each time you do, you will see something that can help your business grow.

Know your references. Before beginning your research, ask yourself what your day's goal is. When you have gathered your information and are ready to leave, go back to that question. See if you have accomplished what you set out to do.

Familiarize yourself with SICs. One of the best ways to start a search for information on a particular group of companies is through the Standard Industrial Classification (SIC). Many business publications organize their contents by SIC numbers or codes, which make it possible to search through directories for relevant information that counts, sorts, lists or compares businesses or their products or services. The goal of the classification is to provide the fullest range of currently available economic activities.

Check directories. Most of the directories referenced later in this chapter can be bought from their publishers. They are usually available in a variety of formats, ranging from computer diskettes to mailing labels. Additionally, many publishers provide free demonstration disks to preview information before you buy. The information you receive is usually the most up-to-date, but be sure to ask when the last update was made just to be safe.

Your Local Libraries

Take a couple of hours to check out your local library. Often, if you call ahead, a reference librarian may be able to give you an overview of business resources. If your local library collection is limited, or if you need more specialized materials, the following larger libraries have extensive business collections:

Arlington Heights Memorial Library
500 N. Dunton Ave.
Arlington Heights, IL 60004
(708) 392-0100
(708) 255-5895 (Night Owl)

Resources for small businesses include a variety of statistical references and directories. Ask about the *Start-Up Index.*

Chicago Public Library
Business/Science/Technology Divisions
400 S. State St.
Chicago, IL 60605
(312) 269-2865 (Information Center)
(312) 747-4400 (Business Center)
(312) 747-4450 (Science/Technology Center)
(312) 747-4136 (For Tours)

This is the largest business resource section in the greater Chicago area.

The Nichols Library
Naperville Public Library
200 W. Jefferson Ave.
Naperville, IL 60540
(708) 355-1540

An excellent resource for both reference and general circulation books for the small business. Though not quite as extensive as Schaumburg or Arlington Heights, it is worth checking.

The Schaumburg Public Library
32 W. Library Ln.
Schaumburg, IL 60194
(708) 885-3373

The second largest business library in the state of Illinois, the Schaumburg library features one of the finest collections of business resources in the Chicago area.

In addition to strong business centers, northern Illinois also has a number of libraries that have extensive collections of federal and state documents. For publications of the Small Business Administration and other government agencies, the following depositories can be quite helpful. To ensure access, it's always best to call first for current hours.

Chicago Public Library
Government Publications Department
400 S. State St.
Chicago, IL 60605
(312) 747-4500

Chicago State University
Douglas Library
95th and King Dr.
Chicago, IL 60628
(312) 995-2341

Northeastern Illinois University Library
5500 N. St. Louis Ave.
Chicago, IL 60625
(312) 583-4050

Northwestern University Library
Government Publications Department
1935 Sheridan Rd.
Evanston, IL 60208
(708) 491-5290

Poplar Creek Public Library
1405 S. Park Ave.
Streamwood, IL 60107
(708) 837-6800

University of Illinois—Chicago
801 S. Morgan
Chicago, IL 60607
(312) 996-2716

Most public libraries are happy to assist you by telephone, which is helpful when you need to verify a fact or determine which library would be best to use for research. Even at night, from 9:00 P.M. until midnight, seven days a week, there is a Night Owl Reference Service supported by selected suburban libraries. The telephone numbers for the various communities are:

■ Resource _____

Name of Resource:	Library Night Owl Service	
Where To Find It:	Addison	(708) 543-3617
	Arlington Hts.	(708) 392-0100
	Barrington	(708) 382-1300
	Bartlett	(708) 837-2855
	Bedford Park	(708) 458-6826

Bellwood	(708) 547-7393
Bridgeview	(708) 458-2880
Brookfield	(708) 485-6917
Des Plaines	(708) 827-5551
Elk Grove	(708) 439-0447
Elmhurst	(708) 279-8696
Highland Park	(708) 432-0216
Lake Forest	(708) 234-0636
Lake Zurich	(708) 438-3433
Lisle	(708) 971-1675
Lombard	(708) 627-0316
Mt. Prospect	(708) 253-5675
Niles	(708) 967-8554
Oak Park	(708) 383-8200
Park Ridge	(708) 825-3123
Riverside	(708) 442-6395
River Forest	(708) 366-5205
Rolling Meadows	(708) 259-6050
Schaumburg	(708) 885-3373
Skokie	(708) 673-7774
Westchester	(708) 562-3573
Westmont	(708) 969-5625
Wheeling	(708) 459-4100
Wilmette	(708) 256-5025
Zion/Benton	(708) 872-4680

Who Could Use It: Anyone

What It Contains: Offers free after-hours information services to the public

Why Use It: Excellent resource when you're working late and need immediate assistance

Company and Industry Research

Company or industry research is essential to any good business plan. Several resources are available:

- *Business Information Directories*   general information on the sources that are important for starting a business
- *Periodical Subject Directories*   help to locate business information in local and national magazines and newspapers
- *Industry Directories*   provide current economic overviews

- *Trade Association Directories*   associations invaluable to the entrepreneur
- *Company Directories*   a major resource for gathering specific company information and compiling lists for marketing and sales
- *Electronic Information*   available through libraries and/or by subscription to provide on-line or CD-ROM information

Business Information Directories

A wealth of small business information is covered in just a few guides. The following sources are good overviews of what is available.

Small Business Information Sources, Joseph C. Schabacker, National Council for Small Business Management Development. Offers general valuable information resources for small businesses.

Small Business Resource Guide, Corporate Services Department, William Rainey Harper College.

Small Business Sourcebook (SBS), Detroit, MI: Gale Research Inc. (updated annually). Expanded and updated coverage of a wide variety of information and assistance. Two Volumes: Volume 1 profiles 194 specific small businesses; Volume 2 covers 39 general small business topics, programs and assistance in each state, local resources and resources not generally found within a library's card catalog — nonprint media, associations, events and commercial agencies. Information is grouped into four sections: Specific Small Business Profiles, General Small Business Topics, State Listings and Federal Government Assistance.

Contains four alphabetized sections, including an index, publication descriptions and sources of information frequently requested on topics organized according to human, economic and community resources. Includes resource information on financial management, legal and government affairs, general management planning, women and minority entrepreneurs, marketing and exporting. This guide is an excellent source of local resource information, for the general Chicagoland area.

Example: You have decided to start a business that will sell computers. You will also provide training for a few, select software packages. You look through the various information directories to obtain an overview of the directories that would be most helpful.

Periodical Subject Directories

The Business Index. Los Altos, CA.: Information Access Co. (updated monthly).

Business Periodicals Index. New York: H.W. Wilson (updated annually).

Small Business Start-Up, edited by Michael Madden, Detroit, MI: Gale Research Inc. (Updated annually). Primarily for start-ups, this guide offers references to periodicals on starting hundreds of small businesses including:

- Accounting/Tax Preparation
- Auto Rental
- Bed and Breakfast
- Children's Day Care
- Computer Maintenance
- Desktop Publishing
- Employment Agency
- Financial Planning
- Home Health Care

- Landscaping Service
- Packaging Service
- Photography Store
- Real Estate Agency
- Restaurant
- Security Systems
- Travel Agency
- Typesetting Business
- Videocassette Rental

If you plan to start a business that is rather unique, this directory could have the resources you are looking for.

Chicago Tribune Index, Chicago, IL: Chicago Tribune Publishing. This index, issued in eight monthly and four quarterly cumulations, as well as a hardbound annual volume, offers abstracts and comprehensive indexing of all significant articles in the newspaper.

Business and financial news is included. Entries are arranged alphabetically, and indexed by subject and under names of corporations, organizations and people. This is a good tool for locating current information about your industry.

Wall Street Journal Index. New York: Dow Jones & Co. (updated monthly with annual cumulations). This publication indexes articles that have appeared in the *Wall Street Journal*.

Wall Street Transcript, published by the *Wall Street Journal*. This index is located in many local library reference sections. It offers a useful source for both specific company information and reviews for an entire industry. It also contains a special section that reviews each industry's key issues and trends.

Example: Now that you have located some potential directories for your computer business, you decide to gather a grouping of timely articles about your field. Through your search, you find many articles on your business. There are even some articles that provide you with marketing ideas you hadn't thought of like using postcards as a way to get new customers. Of greatest importance, however, are the articles that confirm you have found a good business to start.

Industry Directories

Almanac of Business & Industrial Financial Ratios, Englewood Cliffs, NJ; Prentice Hall: (updated annually). This almanac provides comparative financial data on more than 3.6 million United States corporations in 181 fields of business and industry and ranks small, medium and large companies by 22 key financial factors. Identify your company's financial strengths and weakness against those of your competitors. Spot lines of business that might offer new markets for your company. This information is useful when doing financial analysis, accounting, business and sales planning, investment decision making, market research or report writing.

*The Lifestyle Zip Code Analyst,*Wilmette, IL: Standard Rate and Data Service, (708) 256-6067 (updated annually). A wonderful guide to analyze consumer markets, this reference offers an analysis of consumer products broken down by zip code. You could find, for example, the number of households that had computers in a particular zip code. From this information you could then decide where to target your sales efforts.

Predicasts Forecasts, Cleveland, OH: Predicasts, Inc. (updated quarterly). A useful, first place to look for short-term and long-range projections. Good for general market forecasts as well as specific United States industries and products, the book contains information about companies, industries, products and applied technology; arranged alphabetically. Current abstracts cover market data and trends, market research and product development, channels of distribution, sales, management, marketing management and other marketing topics.

This directory gives financial information compiled from hundreds of periodicals, government reports and market studies. It provides another tool for developing financial projections for either products or services or your business in general. Geared toward products and industries, the directory includes forecasts for general economic and demographic characteristics, such as the Gross National Product and the national birth rate.

Note: Predicasts also compiles the *Predicasts' Prompt File* that collects market information from a number of sources. This information is available in either text or statistical form.

Standard & Poor's Industry Report Service, Standard & Poor's Corporation (updated biweekly). This survey gives overviews of nearly 40 industry groups. Each report provides a discussion of industry outlook, a brief guide to recent developments and an overview of major public companies involved in each industry group.

U.S. Industrial Outlook Handbook, Washington, D.C.: U.S. Department of Commerce (updated annually). This publication provides general market data on industry trends and can help you forecast growth rates of a potential market place to see if you have a viable market.

Example: You take a look at the Computer Literature Index and discover reviews of several software packages for which you plan to offer training. You discover the most common problems users have with the programs and make notes to address them in your class. You decide to play this up in your marketing literature promising solutions to those problems as a benefit of your classes. You also locate statistics through the other industrial directories indicating that your market is increasing, on an average, more than 20 percent annually. This will be good information to add to your business plan, and might also help you when you decide to expand your business and when you need a loan. You will have statistical support for your projected growth.

Trade Associations

Business Organizations, Agencies, and Publications Directory, edited by Kay Gil and Donald P. Boyden, 3rd edition, Detroit, MI: Gale Research Inc. (updated between editions by a supplement).

Encyclopedia of Associations. Detroit, MI: Gale Research Inc. (updated annually).

National Trade & Professional Associations of the U.S. and Canada. Washington, D.C.: Columbia Books (updated annually).

With these directories you can locate associations that may be able to provide you with marketing and general business research information. They can also help you stay abreast of the latest industry developments, resolve problems with government or consumers, or get assistance with management education. Association directories offer a compilation of businesses in a particular target market. Keep in mind that associations often produce helpful publications or subscriptions and are great networking centers. For information on associations in the Chicago metropolitan area, see Chapter 12.

Example: You have gathered a tremendous amount of information for your business plan. Now you want to compare your findings with other experts in your field. You decide to find the associations in your area that will support your business. You look through the association directories and locate three that sound interesting. Two of them offer quarterly newsletters and annual surveys of your potential market. You decide to join one of the associations that is close to your new place of business.

Company Directories

Some of the most important *national* business directories are:

Directory of Corporate Affiliations. Skokie, IL: National Register Publishing Co., (updated annually with bimonthly supplements). This directory will help you gather accurate marketing information about potential customers and competitors.

National Directory of Addresses and Telephone Numbers. Kirkland, WA (updated annually). More than 210,000 listings of top corporations, United States and foreign government agencies are listed here, as well as nonprofit organizations, international trade contacts and embassies.

Standard & Poor's Register of Corporations. New York: Standard & Poor's Corporation (updated annually with monthly supplements). Although designed primarily for investors, this directory can provide a good overview of your marketplace. The "Basic Analysis" section offers an overview of trends and issues under broad industry category headings.

Thomas Register of American Manufacturers. New York: Thomas Publishing Company (updated quarterly and annually). A valuable resource that helps you to identify suppliers, potential customers and competitors. The directory is divided into three sections: "Products and Services," a list of companies according to their products; "Company Profile," an alphabetical listing of companies along with their products; and "Catalog File," information on companies and the catalogs they produce. This book can be helpful when you are developing the marketing and operations sections of your business plan.

Wards Business Directory of U.S. Private and Public Companies. Detroit, MI: Gale Research Inc. (updated annually). A list of more than 133,000 companies, since 1960 this five-volume set has been considered the leading source for hard-to-find information on private companies. The most recent edition contains information on America's smallest companies with sales of less than $50,000. Extensive financial information is provided about companies under the headings of *Total Assets, Gross Billings* and *Operating Revenues.*

There are several guides to metropolitan Chicago and Illinois business, including:

Chicago and Cook County Marketing Directory. Chicago, IL (updated annually). Up to 30 facts on all manufacturers as well as the major service businesses in the county. Listings include: company name and address, key company executives, product description, SIC code, number of employees, square footage, county and year established. Up to 30 facts are included on all manufacturers, which can be helpful when qualifying potential customers.

Chicago Business Area Directory. Omaha, NE: American Directory Publishing Co., Inc.

Section 1 contains businesses by yellow page business listing, and businesses listed for the entire Chicago metropolitan area.

Section 2 contains manufacturers listed by city and SIC Code and includes Chicago area manufacturers with ten or more employees. Chicago area businesses are listed alphabetically by city in Section 3. Each business appears only once.

Doing Business in Chicago , Jeffrey P. Levine, Homewood, IL: Business One-Irwin, 1991 (updated regularly). This book contains comprehensive information on 750 private, mutual, foreign, nonprofit and subsidiary companies in Chicago and helps you identify potential markets for your product or service. Probably most helpful when preparing annual marketing plans, this reference can provide you with important information about your competitors.

First Chicago Guide: Major Publicly Held Corporations & Financial Institutions Headquartered in Illinois. Deerfield, IL: Scholl Communications, Inc. (updated annually). For those small businesses marketing to larger businesses, this directory can be useful for targeting potential customers.

Illinois Industrial Directory. Twinsburg, OH: Harris Publishing (published annually in cooperation with the Illinois Chamber of Commerce). A reference that contains extensive information about Illinois companies, including: name, address, county, phone number, SIC, number of employees, size, contact names.

Illinois Manufacturers Directory. Evanston, IL: Manufacturers News, Inc. (updated annually).

Divided into six sections:

Buyers Guide   A list of companies by product or industrial service that can help you to find services, purchase products or locate an Illinois business in a specific industry.

Alphabetical Section   A listing of Illinois manufacturers and processors by company name, address, phone number and city where the business can be located in the geographical listings.

Geographical   A complete information source that provides city, telephone number, fax, toll-free telephone number and mailing address plus key information on personnel, product, size, parent company, computer used, distribution, date established and annual sales.

Standard Industrial Code (SIC)   A listing of manufacturers and processors by SIC.

Computer Section   A listing of computers by brand name and the name and city of all Illinois companies using that equipment.

Chicago Zip Code   A listing of companies in the 606 zip code prefix.

Extra: For the first time, this directory lists annual sales figures and brand names of products companies are using. Also, information on ownership has been added to many listings, as well as a new line that indicates whether the business is privately or publicly owned and the legal status of the business (i.e., corporation, sole proprietorship, etc.)

Illinois Services Directory. Evanston, IL: Manufacturers News, Inc. (published annually)

Alphabetic   Illinois service companies are listed by company name. Listings include address, phone number and city where company can be located in the geographical listings.

Geographical   Illinois service companies are listed by city or town with telephone number, fax number, toll-free number and mailing address plus key information on personnel, product, size, parent company, computer used, distribution, date established and annual sales.

Parent Company   Each company's home office is listed alphabetically followed by its subsidiaries.

SIC   Numerical list of Illinois service companies by SIC classification including address, telephone number, number of employees and city where company is located in geographical listings.

LeadSource. N. Olmsted, OH (updated annually). In addition to basic company information (e.g., contact name, address, SIC code, etc.,) this resource provides the number of employees and years in business, primarily sorted by zip code. Also listed are type of business location—sole office, home office, branch office or franchise office. As the editors of *LeadSource* state, "Out of 1,000 key executives in an industry in a given year, only 453—less than half—stay on the same job in the same company and at the same location." *LeadSource* is a starting place for creating personalized direct mailing, telemarketing campaigns or for generating new sales leads.

Metropolitan Chicago Major Employers Directory. Chicago: Chicago Association of Commerce and Industry (updated annually). Another compilation of larger businesses, both publicly and privately held, in Chicago. Again, a publication of interest to those who want detailed and comprehensive information on the larger companies in Chicago.

Note: Company directories are a great source for sales leads. According to several recent surveys, the average sales call costs around $229. This amount represents an increase of approximately 222 percent over the last 10 years. Another survey shows that more than 64 percent of all sales calls are made to the wrong person. Combine these two surveys, and you have a very good reason to take the extra time needed to find the right companies and company contacts to market your business. Keep in mind that different directories contain a variety of information, so cross-referencing is very useful.

Example: You are working on the marketing portion of your business plan, and it's time to create a sales plan. You decide to spend the first six months of business sending letters to your target market, following up with a call and hopefully with an appointment. You compile your first list using a variety of the directories listed above.

Electronic Information

Electronic information has been growing in importance in recent years, even though it is not cheap. Many libraries have access to a variety of business databases, and some have CD-ROM units available in their reference areas. CD-ROMs look just like computers and act like computers, but millions of bits of information are stored on a "silver" disc similar to musical compact discs. Learn what is available at your library. Often an expensive electronic search can be arranged by the library at no cost or for a very nominal charge.

An example of an invaluable electronic service found in many metropolitan libraries is:

General Business File The general business file is a CD-ROM database that integrates major sources of business and company information. Available through InfoTrak (a computerized database found at many local libraries) this file integrates major sources of business and company information, including:

- reference articles from 800 business, management, trade journals and newspapers;
- directory listings for over 100,000 companies (90,000 of these are privately owned), ranking the top companies in cities and states;
- full news text releases, enabling you to obtain late-breaking company news;
- information such as company and industry reports, detailed financials and forecasts, summaries and analysis on companies, products and industries.

Samples of on-line computer databases that many libraries have access to are:

Dow Jones News/Retrieval
Local library or PO Box 300
Princeton, NJ 08543-0300
(609) 452-1511 or (800) 522-3567

The number one electronic news source for financial professionals provides stock exchange updates, full text and abstracted information from financial publications. A complete range of real-time and historical data can be downloaded to spreadsheets. Charges are $2 to $3 per minute during prime time.

Dun's Direct Access, a Dun and Bradstreet Company
Local library or 3 Sylvan Way
Parsippany, NJ 07054-3896
(800) 654-7834

Approximately nine million companies are searchable by industry, geographic location, zip code, sales volume and number of employees. Updated daily.

The Chicago Public Library has a separate computer center that can assist with business research:

Computer-Assisted Reference Center
The Chicago Public Library
400 S. State St.
Chicago, IL 60605
(312) 747-4470

This fee-based information retrieval service expands the reference services of the library and accesses nearly 500 databases. Computer searches provide immediate on-line display and a print-out of references to material such as journal and newspaper articles, technical reports, conference proceedings, dissertations, government documents and books. This information is invaluable for market research.

There are also private computer services that you can access by paying a fee:

Business Infoline (900) 896-0000 ($3 first minute/$1.50 each additional minute)

For further information call: (402) 593-4593 (Monday through Friday 8:00 AM to 5:00 PM central time)

Operators are available to assist in accessing a database of 9.2 million businesses in the United States compiled from the yellow pages. The service provides listings of types and locations of businesses with information on mailing address, SIC code, sales volume, owner/manager's name and number of employees. Use this service to obtain information on specific businesses.

CompuServe Information Service
5000 Arlington Centre Blvd.
PO Box 20212
Columbus, OH 43220
To order service:
Dept. L Box 477
PO Box 18161
Columbus, OH 43272-4630
(800) 848-8990

Research and networking opportunities are offered, as well as access to specialized databases via computer, modem and telephone. Basic usage, Users Guide, a Quick Reference Booklet and monthly *Online Today* are included in the one-time membership charge of $39.95. Connect charges are based on your modem's speed, with communication surcharges for most at local call rate. Executive Option/Professional Connection is available. **New Service:** CompuServe now offers a special package with a low monthly fee of $7.95, plus a one-time membership fee. This package allows you use of popular options such as news, sports, weather, reference materials and E-mail service of 60 messages a month. Additional services are also available at nominal additional charges.

GEnie (GE Network for Information Exchange)
401 N. Washington St.
Mail Stop MC5A
Rockville, MD 20850
(800) 638-9636 (voice line)
(800) 638-8369 (modem sign-up line)

This service is a bit more difficult to use than CompuServe, but also less expensive ($5-$10 per hour nonprime-time fee.) There are more than 200,000 current subscribers who have access to a wide range of business and computer support groups, including the Home-Office Small Business Roundtable and a variety of other professional and software roundtables.

Fedix and Molis
(800) 25FEDIX or (800) 62/MOLIS—(Call this number for more information.)
FEDIX is a dial-up, on-line service providing access to a collection of databases of federal government research and education-related information. The databases include agency contacts, scholarships, fellowships and grants, available research equipment, procurement notices from the *Commerce Business Daily*, *Federal Register* and other sources and current events within participating agencies.

MOLIS is the Minority On-Line Information Service that can be used to gain information on Black and Hispanic colleges and universities, federal agency education, research, equipment and employment opportunities.

Participating agencies include: the Department of Energy, Commerce, Education, and Housing and Urban Development;

the Office of Naval Research, National Aeronautics and Space Administration; Federal Aviation Administration; National Science Foundation and U.S. Agency for International Development.

Both services offer free information about business opportunities and can be contacted 24 hours a day.

Prodigy Interactive Personal Service
Prodigy Services Co.
445 Hamilton Ave.
White Plaines, NY 10601
(914) 993-8000
(800) 284-5933 ext. 205 for information or a sign-up kit

Prodigy is available for $9.95 per month. Although shopping is emphasized, the service also features late-breaking news, home-business advice and computer and software reviews (courtesy of *Home-Office Computing*), on-line business and financial experts, financial services, and more.

Note: Just as you are able to find volumes of information manually, you can find even more electronically. The Information Age has introduced a wide variety of electronic information bases that can be retrieved quickly and cost effectively if you take the time to do some preliminary legwork and paperwork.

Most databases charge both annual fees and usage fees. Therefore, if your search request is broad, your costs increase. By taking the time to focus your request, you can keep your initial costs down.

The main advantage of looking at resources available in an on-line database is the timeliness of the information. Many directories, even if they have a copyright date in the current year, are six months or more out of date once you have access to them. Databases, on the other hand, are updated daily, giving you the most recent information available on a particular topic. Many entrepreneurs, especially those who are creating new products or services, could benefit from the information generated from an electronic search.

Example: You have the librarian at your local library search information on three large companies you are planning to do business with. You find out that one of the companies is planning to open a new office in a town near you. You make a preliminary check with the company's human resources department and find out that they have not yet thought about computer training for the personnel that will be housed at the new location. You prepare a proposal for this job prior to your meeting with the company.

Research Help

Two additional resources for gathering valuable business information are the information broker and the consultant. The major difference between the two is that information brokers provide information in its raw form allowing their clients to make necessary deductions and decisions while consultants help their clients do something with the raw data. Charges for these services usually start at $75 per hour.

Information brokers can provide you with a bibliography or a bibliography with an abstract (which typically costs a bit more) of each resource item you are having them research. You can also request *document retrieval* or *document delivery*, which provides the document in its entirety.

To locate an information broker who can provide the assistance you require, take a look at the *Burwell Directory of Information Brokers* (Burwell Enterprises, Inc.—updated annually). If this directory is unavailable, contact your reference librarian. The annual *Directory of Fee-Based Information Services*, published by Helen Burwell, is another good resource, as are the American Society for Information Services (ASIS) in Washington, D.C. and the Association of Independent Information Professionals (AIIP) in Milwaukee, Wisconsin. Finally, a rather inexpensive resource is The Wisconsin Innovation Center of Whitewater, Wisconsin, (414) 472-1365 or (414) 472-1600. Business students and technical consultants from this small business development center run by the University of Wisconsin—Whitewater provide clients with market feasibility reports and ad hoc research. Feasibility reports that include competitive analyses and overall market risk ratings are generated in 30 to 90 days for a reasonable fee. This research would be particularly helpful to inventors, product-based companies and anyone who wants to analyze a particular market's potential prior to making a substantial investment.

Small Business Resource Books

We have filled this text with references to books on specific topics. Most of the books we list are available through your local library, yet there may be some that you choose to buy for your personal library. Contact your local bookstore for assistance.

Following is a list of books we recommend:

Fuld, Leonard M. *Competitor Intelligence: How To Get It—How To Use It*. New York: John Wiley & Sons, Inc., 1985. A good book for obtaining an understanding of the basics of competitor intelligence, why it is useful, how to use it effectively, etc. The language is simple and useful for novice researchers.

Luck, David J. *Marketing Research*. Englewood Cliffs, NJ: Prentice-Hall, 1987.

Mancuso, Joseph. *The Small Business Resource Guide*. New York: Prentice Hall/Simon & Schuster, 1989. This guide contains business advice and spicy anecdotes amid short descriptions of associations, consultants, directories and government agencies. It refers you to 600 sources that will provide answers, references, people and other informational listings.

Mayer, Martin. *Markets: Who Plays, Who Risks, Who Gains, Who Loses*. New York: Norton, 1988.

Mitchell, Arnold. *The Nine American Lifestyles: Who We Are and Where We Are Going*. New York: Warner Books, 1984. A book that categorizes the United States population into nine different lifestyles and offers pointers on how to appeal to people within each group.

Porter, Michael E. *Competitive Advantage*. New York: Free Press, 1986. A discussion of how a firm can identify its competitive advantage and gain a profitable position within its market.

■ Five ■

Assessing Costs and Needs

■

Starting a business *does not* work like this: 1) you decide you want to start a business; 2) you find a bank or other governmental funding source; 3) you tell them how much money you want; and 4) they give it to you. Instead, the scenario is a lot more like this: 1) you decide you want to start a business; 2) you try to get money—at least six to twelve months worth of operating expenses; 3) you find that the very few funding agencies willing to lend you money expect you to put up collateral—your home, your car, etc.; 4) you decide *not* to take that risk; and 5) you end up starting with little or no money hoping your sales will pay for monthly expenses and expansion. Beware! Lack of capital is the number one reason small businesses fail. Save at least enough money to cover six to twelve months of projected operating expenses before you start.

Start-Up Costs

The first step in planning your business is to take a realistic look at what your costs will be. Start a list, and jot down every expense category that comes to mind. From this, set up a work sheet containing an estimate for each item. Following are a few categories that should be in your calculations:

Location   Where you locate your business will strongly influence your cost of doing business and your success in the market. Small businesses have more options today than ever before. A great way to save money is to work out of your home. Assume the aura of a more stable business by using a mail box address service that provides you with a recognizable business address. You may require space in an office or industrial center. You might even consider locating your newly organized business in an *incubator*, designed to provide a supportive environment, as well as the materials and consultative guidance. Incubators can reduce start-up costs through the sharing of resources and overhead. Additional information on incubators can be found in Chapter 9.

Your Business Plan   Whether you write your own business plan or decide to hire a specialist to assist you, there will be costs involved for researching, writing and printing. We recommend that you spend the time and dollars necessary to develop a *realistic* plan. Chapter 6 describes the creation of a business plan in detail.

Start-Up Fees   As a new business owner, you can expect to pay the start-up fees that we discussed in Chapter 2.

- *Attorney's fees*   These can include costs of incorporation or drawing up partnership agreements. Whether you plan to remain on your own, take on a partner or form a corporation, we advise that you see an attorney *prior to* start-up.
- *Accounting fees*   Whether or not you will need monthly record-keeping services, we advise you to see an accountant prior to start-up.

Supplies   Costs for the materials of your profession must be anticipated: stationery, business cards, telephone system, answering and fax machines, photocopier and personal computer.

Office Furnishings and Equipment   You will need a desk, chair, filing cabinet(s), bookshelves and lighting. Do what you can to reduce these costs at first by buying secondhand. See the Appendix for a list of sources.

Insurance   Insure your equipment and your office separately. Do not include the equipment under your existing homeowner's policy unless you use a *home office rider* or addendum. Purchase a policy that covers replacement costs. You will also need an umbrella liability policy to cover things like customers getting hurt on your property.

Miscellaneous Expenses   Add a 20 percent financial cushion for emergencies.

Working Capital   You must pay yourself to cover personal and family bills. You should have enough in the bank or in *liquid assets* (mutual funds, pension funds, stocks and bonds), to cover business expenses for three to six months.

Starting a Business at Home

Many businesses are quite appropriately conducted out of homes. Free-lance writing or editing businesses, for example, do not require an outside office. Sometimes a business is started at home as a way to control costs. As the business grows and space demands increase, the owner has both the confidence and the cash to make a lease commitment. More and more people are setting up offices in their homes, and a number of resources are available to help them.

■ Resources _____

Name of Resource:	Illinois Bell Work-at-Home Infoline
Where To Find It:	(800) 274-5669 (Call to order free copies of the publications listed below.)
What It Contains:	*Work-at-Home Catalog* A listing of the most advanced products available to meet the needs of the home office professional, from telephones and computer modems to fax and answering machines.
	The Home Office Reference Manual If you have a computer modem or are thinking of buying one, Illinois Bell has a reference manual that takes the guesswork out of buying, installing and using a modem.

"Work-at-Home" Newsletter Illinois Bell's bimonthly newsletter contains plenty of homeworker news and tips designed to make working at home more productive and fun.

Name of Resource: The Work-at-Home Planning Center
Where To Find It: 230 W. Washington
Chicago, IL 60606
(800) 232-0285
What It Contains: A hands-on demonstration of home office communication equipment and free advice from a Work-at-Home Specialist. Hours are 8:30 A.M. to 5:00 P.M., Monday through Friday.

Name of Resource: Work-at-Home Specialists
Where To Find It: (800) 232-0285
What It Contains: Speak directly to a knowledgeable, experienced specialist who understands your concerns and is prepared to answer questions about your communication needs. Consultants offer advice that can help you work more effectively, covering topics such as transmitting data over local telephone lines or new telecommunications products and services.

Name of Resource: Illinois Bell Seminars for the Home Office Professional
Where To Find It: To register call (800) 435-4680 between 8:00 A.M. and 5:00 P.M. , Monday through Friday, or request a registration form and mail or fax it to (800) 437-7530
What It Contains: These seminars are designed for experienced homeworkers, as well as those whose businesses are still in the developmental stage. The seminars address such issues as:
- Getting started   ▪ Financing
- Increasing efficiency ▪ Promoting sales
- Enhancing your image

Name of Resource: Ameritech Services Small Business Publications
Where To Find It: (800) 242-8580

What It Contains: From time to time, Ameritech offers special publications for entrepreneurs. Call the number above to be put on a mailing list for future publications and receive a copy of *A Guide to Increasing Business with Existing Customers.*

--- ∎

Buying an Existing Business

If you have capital, you might consider buying a business. Entrepreneurs who start or purchase businesses and succeed in running them profitably possess a hardiness, tenacity and willingness to risk not inherent in everyone. According to Nancy Dodd McCann, president of The Fordham Group, Inc., a Barrington, Illinois business consultancy specializing in acquisitions: "While franchises provide support, owners of new businesses must understand fully the businesses they purchase and possess the skills and personality necessary to operate them effectively. More than assets, a potential stream of profits, a building housing some process called work or the fulfillment of a life-long dream, a purchased business is a complex organism of many living parts: a strategic plan, a market position and reputation, a technology, assets, debts, equity and people. A particular chemistry or culture makes it go or not go."

Six distinct cycles surface during the purchase process. Far too many individuals start at cycle three, however, not realizing that cycles one and two are critical for long-term success. The six cycles are as follows:

1) Determining one's suitability for the type of business ownership
2) Understanding possible strategies for buying a business and selecting one; setting parameters for the purchase
3) Locating potential businesses for sale
4) Evaluating *all* aspects of the business, including "due diligence"
5) Negotiating and completing the purchase of the business
6) Planning and implementing a successful transition of ownership

Specificity and analysis during these cycles pays off. For example, one could be unsuitable for sole business ownership but suitable for a partnership with someone of complementary skills or as a joint decision maker. Strategies are critical. The cost of buying a business should never exceed the cost of starting one yourself, unless lack of time or skills are factors. Setting parameters for the purchase will ensure that you don't fall in love with a business that doesn't meet your needs. The use of a career counselor who specializes in strategy development within acquisitions, rather than a business broker (often called a mergers and acquisitions consultant), will help you toward a positive outcome. Counselors of both types may be available through small business institutes at community colleges. However, if you are not knowledgeable in acquisitions, you should request a referral to qualified business consultants rather than brokers. After the parameters are understood, the business of locating a business commences. This is the time to involve a business broker, almost always required in a seller's market. Brokers work on commission from the sale of a business, presenting businesses to the most likely buyers and/or those who pay them a fee for a search—an advance that is deducted from the sales commission.

Brokers know where to find businesses for sale, the current market and going prices. While accountants often look primarily at *asset* value, brokers regularly appraise businesses on *market* value. Additionally, brokers understand sellers and can often negotiate a successful purchase where a neophyte cannot.

Potential buyers should hire professionals who perform due diligence. This should include a full investigation of not only financial and legal concerns, but also the quality of the products, customers, employees and management. Since confidentiality must be maintained during the prospective sale, potential owners must often negotiate with the potential seller for permission to contact suppliers and customers, or pay for a market research study. A trained interviewer specializing in mergers and acquisitions should evaluate any management expected to remain with the business. This evaluation can provide a potential buyer with a better understanding of specifically how the business operates. It is the lack of information prior to purchase—mostly nonfinancial in nature—that is the most common cause of subsequent business failures.

A business broker, or merger and acquisition consultant, will negotiate purchases. Even if you don't use a broker to locate a business, you may purchase their services for the negotiation process. Before the purchase is consummated, a buyer should formulate a plan to manage through the transition. A merger consultant specializing in assimilations, as well as the other phases, can prevent major problems from developing.

Business ownership is a viable option, but locating the *right* business can take more than 18 months—after the preliminary strategy is developed and before negotiations begin. The entire cycle may well take three years, a cycle longer than most neophytes realize when beginning.

Checklist for Buying a Business

Ask yourself the following questions:

- What types of businesses match your skills and personality?
- What level of risk can you live with?
- For what strategic reason are you purchasing a business?
- Are you sure you know the real reason the owner wants to sell this business?
- Have you talked with other business owners who might know the current owner in order to find out what they think of the business?
- What is the image of the business in the marketplace?
- Have you spoken with the business's suppliers?
- Have you spoken with current customers of the business?
- Is the technology of the business current?
- What is the business's value?
- If there is a building involved, is it in good shape?
- If there is stock, is it in good condition?
- If there is a lease involved, is there a possibility of transferring the lease to you?
- Have you compared the cost of buying this business with the cost of starting a similar one yourself?
- How will you determine the price you will pay?
- Have you made a complete list of all the advantages and disadvantages of buying this business?
- Have you talked with the owner about possible financing assistance?
- Have you spoken with an attorney?

- Have you done your research to see if this is the kind of business that offers growth potential and is right for you?

■ Resource

Name of Resource:	Association for Corporate Growth
Where To Find It:	4350 Di Paolo Center
	Dearlove Rd., Ste. C
	Glenview, IL 60025
	(708) 966-1777
Who Could Use It:	Anyone interested in locating a specialist in most phases of acquisition
Name of Resource:	*Illinois Business Directory*
	American Directory Publishing Company
Where To Find It:	Your local library reference section
What It Contains:	Look under the heading *Business Brokers*—a compilation of the *Yellow Pages* for the entire state
Why Use It:	Saves looking through separate *Yellow Pages* to locate information

■

Publications

Coltman, Michael, *Buying and Selling a Small Business.* Self-Counsel Press, 1989.

Directory of Merger and Acquisition Firms and Professionals. Business One-Irwin.

Joseph, R.; Nekoranec, A.; Steffens, C., *How To Buy a Business.* Dearborn Financial Publishing, 1993.

Kalien, Laurence H., *How To Get Rich Buying Bankrupt Companies.* Carol Communications, 1989.

Mancuso, Joseph, *Buying a Business for Very Little Cash.* Prentice Hall, 1990.

Pratt, Shannon P., *Valuing a Business.* Dow Jones-Irwin, 1989.

Buying a Franchise

Buying franchises offers a viable method for many to enter the world of business ownership. By aligning with an established franchise, you can benefit from the expertise, advice and business acumen of a parent organization. Franchises generally provide support mechanisms, as well as the research and many of the solutions to business decisions that often torment new businesses. Franchises offer everything from market research and site selection to supply sources for promotional materials and products. In some cases they may provide management guidance in day-to-day operations. The purchaser of the franchise (the franchisee) pays the parent franchise company (the franchisor), a base franchise fee plus a percentage of profits in exchange for permission to use the name of the business and its standardized service or products. Additionally, the franchise agreement gives the franchisee the right to sell products or services in a specified geographic area.

There are many advantages to buying a franchise operation, including:

- Use of an established name that offers faster recognition of your business and a faster return on your initial investment
- Comparatively low franchise fees, especially for certain types of businesses that have been created to fill new market niches (diaper delivery services, senior day care and pet sitting)
- Lower marketing costs because of shared publicity
- Lower supply costs because of volume discounts when many franchisees are purchasing the same supplies

Disadvantages of Franchising

A word of caution. It is critical that you research the franchise market very carefully. You need to know and understand every detail of the franchise business you eventually select. There are excellent franchises available—and there are some that are not particularly reliable. Keep in mind that opening a franchise operation is, in effect, forming a partnership with another company. You can benefit from the assets that company brings to the partnership, and you can also suffer from any negatives. The negatives include:

- *Conforming to operation standards* When you buy a franchise, more often than not you are buying a standardized way of operating. Many entrepreneurs end up feeling constrained by these standards.

- *Profit sharing*   As mentioned earlier, many franchises charge a royalty on a percentage of gross sales. This ultimately comes out of your profits. Sometimes this fee is required *whether you make a profit or not.*
- *Other restrictions*   Some franchises restrict you from meeting your competitor's prices, adding or dropping certain inventory. Your contract may contain other restrictions that are particular to the franchise you are purchasing.

As always, think through the entire process. Ask questions. If you don't ask the right questions, you won't get the information you need to make a wise decision. As we've recommended several times, seek the advice of an attorney, *before* you negotiate a contract. If possible, use your attorney *during* the negotiation process rather than after you've gone through the contract. Following are resources that may be of particular help when looking at purchasing a franchise:

■ Resources _____

Name of Resource:	*Annual Franchise 500*
	Entrepreneur Magazine
Where To Find It:	*Entrepreneur* Subscription Dept.,
	PO Box 50368
	Boulder, CO 80321-0368
	(800) 284-5534
	Check the magazine rack of your local bookstore.
What It Contains:	Lists information on 500 leading franchise operations. Updated annually.
Name of Resource:	Franchise Disclosure
Where To Find It:	Attorney General Franchise Division
	500 S. Second
	Springfield, IL 62706
	(217) 782-4465
Who Could Use It:	Anyone wanting to purchasing a franchise
What It Contains:	The *Franchise Disclosure Act* requires a franchisor to register with the Illinois

Attorney General and provide a franchisee with detailed information regarding their relationship, the details of the contract, the prior business experience of the franchisor and other information relevant to the franchise offered for sale.

Why Use It: To ensure that you are purchasing a legitimate franchise

When To Use It: Prior to signing any documentation relative to the purchase of a franchise

Name of Resource: *The Franchise Annual*
Where To Find It: Info Franchise News
728 Center St.
PO Box 550
Lewiston, NY 14092
(716) 754-4669

Who Could Use It: Anyone interested in exploring opportunities in franchising

What It Contains: Names of companies, locations, whom to contact, description of operation, capital requirements and other data

When To Use It: Anytime prior to setting up a franchise arrangement

Name of Resource: *Handbook of Successful Franchising* by Mark P. Friedlander and Gene Gurney, (Liberty Hall Press, 1990)
Where To Find It: Libraries and bookstores
What It Contains: Information on 1,500 franchises. The book offers a brief summary of terms, requirements and conditions under which each franchise is available.

Name of Resource: International Franchise Association
Where To Find It: 1350 New York Ave. N.W., Ste. 900
Washington, DC 20005
(202) 628-8000

What It Contains: This Association holds expos around the country (Chicago's expo is usually held in early September) and offers a bimonthly newsletter called *Franchise Opportunities* and a *Franchise Opportunities Guide*.

Name of Resource:	Women in Franchising
Where To Find It:	175 N. Harbor Dr. #405
	Chicago, IL 60601
	(800) 222-4943
Who Could Use It:	Women or minorities interested in franchising and networking
What It Contains:	National membership organization for women interested franchising

Publications

Bond, Robert E. *Source Book of Franchise Opportunities.* Dow Jones-Irwin, 1990. Covers the history, financial start-up and training support for 3,750 American and Canadian American franchise opportunities.

Evaluating Franchise Opportunities, Use the document request form located in *The One Stop Business Start-Up Kit* available through the Illinois Business Hotline (800) 252-2923.

Franchise and Business Opportunities Program, Federal Trade Commission, Washington, DC 20580. (202) 326-2222. Write for information about enforcement of FTC Rule 346, which governs what a franchisor must disclose to a potential franchisee. Request the FTC's Consumer Bulletin No. 4, "Advice for Persons Who Are Considering an Investment in a Franchise Business."

Budgets and Bookkeeping

Once you have been in business for more than a year—preferably two years—you will create a financial history that will offer the basis for possible commercial financing. A lender will evaluate your financial stability when considering a loan to your business. Therefore, take the time to nurture your business by watching what you spend in the early years.

Organizing Your Finances—Five Steps toward Financial Security

1) Consider obtaining the advice of a financial planner to help organize your financial goals, or take a management accounting course at a local university.
2) Draw up a budget that is realistic, and stick to it. Make sure you incorporate sporadic expenses, such as: legal fees,

hardware and software, club dues and miscellaneous advertising costs.

3) Keep organized records of payments and expenses. Keeping good books saves you time and money. Your checkbook is a handy database of expenditures. Avoid spending cash.

4) If you have extra money, consider saving a portion and using the additional earnings for more marketing, especially in the early stages of business.

5) Have your accountant review your earnings on a quarterly basis to help you organize your financial plan.

Your books should enable you to do more than just keep records. They should tell you what percentage of profit you are making; whether you are charging enough or spending too much; whether you are directing your energies in certain business areas wisely, prepared for a temporary (or long-term) downturn in business; collecting all the monies owed you and many other details that can keep you on top of your cash flow. Each business has its own requirements concerning keeping of books, with much depending upon the form of the business and the specific industry requirements. There are a number of excellent software packages that can help you.

Cash Flow

When all is said and done, cash flow is the life blood of every business. It is cash flow that determines a business's health and its ability to sustain over the long run. Your first priority is to get as much cash as possible coming into the business, and as little going out, as quickly as you can.

Refuse business and deals that don't produce enough profit. Many business owners have discovered that they work just as hard for a $25 customer as they do for a $2,500 customer. Your first responsibility is to sustain yourself and your business so that you can continue to be available to offer your services or products. If you can't pay the bills, you won't be around to do business.

Entrepreneurs need to establish very clearly their expectations concerning payment. No matter how desirable a specific job, if you don't get paid, you've hurt yourself and your business. Those who negotiate and sign contracts for major projects have less trouble than those who don't. It's also important that you be very selective about whom you will work with. It's a waste of your time and energy to work with customers who don't honor their commitments. Tom Barnicle, CPA, a partner in the firm of John Hauter and Associates recommends, "Establish terms of payment up front to prevent questions being asked later. Also, don't be afraid to ask for money that is owed to you. You did the work; you deserve to get paid. Not asking for payment is a sign that you don't think you were worth it."

When times get tough, and you have to stretch beyond your means for a while, you must always keep the doors of communication open. Tell your creditors and suppliers that you are running a very tight ship. Let them know what you're doing to correct the situation. They'll respect you for your openness. It's only when they find you becoming inaccessible that they begin to question your sincerity and anticipate the probability that you'll leave them hanging.

Be willing to do any work you can yourself until it becomes counterproductive. At that point, it is better to do what you do best and "hire out the rest." When you reach the point where you think you are ready to expand, look at temporaries, consultants or independent contractors (see your accountant before you hire one) before hiring employees.

When paying your bills, keep the following order of priority in mind:

- Payroll
- Taxes (payroll, state, federal, social security, unemployment, etc.)
- Bank loans
- Rent and utilities
- Suppliers
- All other expenses

Payroll taxes should be of particular concern to entrepreneurs. Penalties for noncompliance are severe. Even if you are incorporated, you can be personally liable and hit with a 100 percent penalty for nonpayment.

■ Six ■

The Business Plan

■

Business plans are usually written to secure financing. Few, if any, funding sources—banks, venture capitalists, angels or even family members—will lend money without a written plan. They all want to know when and how you will pay back the money you want to borrow. A smart entrepreneur also understands that a business plan is an important foundation for a business's day-to-day action plan. Whatever reason you may have had before, after reading this chapter, we hope you will see the importance of a written business plan.

David H. Bangs, Jr., in his book *The Business Planning Guide*, suggests three major reasons for going to the trouble of writing a business plan:

1) The process of putting a business plan together, including the thought you put in before beginning to write it, forces you to take an objective, critical, unemotional look at your business project in its entirety.
2) The finished product—your business plan—is an operating tool that, if properly used, will help you manage your business and work effectively toward its success.

3) The completed business plan communicates your ideas to others and provides the basis for your financing proposal.

Take the time to sit down and put on paper the basic *Who, What, Why, Where, When* and *How* of your business. This chapter will define the basic components of a business plan, while offering an overview of the resources available to help you write one.

What a Plan Can Do

A business plan can open doors for you. It creates, perhaps, the only solid evidence that you can do what you say you can do. How do you create such a plan? You can use one of the books or publications referenced in this chapter, buy a software program designed to aid in the creation of business plans, or find an individual or firm that specializes in writing plans. Check the Index of this book under *Entrepreneurial Consultants*, or contact your local small business development center to locate a specialist. Rhonda Abrams, in her book, *The Successful Business Plan* (Oasis Press), sets forth the five fundamental steps to the business plan process:

1) Lay out your basic business concept.
2) Gather data on the feasibility and specifics of your concept.
3) Focus and refine the concept based on your data.
4) Outline the specifics of your business.
5) Put your plan into compelling form.

Research and develop all the components of your plan. Take the time to know your market. These steps will greatly improve the quality and success of your plan. This is the basic marketing research that will help you better understand your industry and how your business fits in.

Jill Johnson of Johnson Consulting in Minneapolis, states: "One of the most crucial elements of any plan is going to be tying your projected revenues to your expenses." Johnson also emphasizes the need for businesses to revisit their business plans as they enter the second critical stage of business development that usually occurs when the business is three to five years old. She adds, "You will be more sophisticated then. It is the best time to go back and rethink your vision."

A lot of businesses neglect long-range planning. Johnson suggests you combine this with long-range, strategic planning.

An ongoing business plan helps you to see new opportunities and manage growth.

Finally, Johnson notes that the written plan helps you with one of the most important and critical areas to your success—pricing. Many entrepreneurs do not take the time to find out what is competitive in the market. It is extremely difficult to compete on price.

Johnson explains, "If you deeply discount your numbers, you will have nothing left for cash or savings. What you have done is discount yourself out of the market. We as a nation have created an image that the more expensive the better. We have conditioned ourselves to believe that if we get it for free or cheap it is not very good. You can lose clients when your low prices decrease your credibility as a valued source of business. This is especially true with service businesses. I recommend people come close to the middle of the price ranges you discover through researching your competition."

The Critical Dozen

All the elements of the business plan can be identified relatively easily with diligent research and by giving careful thought to the following questions *before* you start:

1) Who are you? What is your business idea? Why do you think this idea will work? What do you expect to accomplish? How will you do it? What does the future look like? This becomes your Executive Summary.
2) What is your reason for starting this business? This is your Mission Statement.
3) What is your philosophy? What are the driving forces that guide and motivate you?
4) What do you expect to achieve and when? If you don't have a goal, you cheat yourself; you have nothing to strive for, no reason to get there and—quite frankly, you don't even have the commitment to make it happen.
5) Do you have a business name; a structure (i.e., sole proprietor, corporation, etc.)?
6) What are you selling? This is very important, and reflects back to your Mission Statement. For example, if you are going to sell can openers, are you selling them as tools that cut metal cans so you can get food out? Are you selling

speed and efficiency so that the user can get on to other, more important activities? Or are you selling the prestige of owning a one-of-a-kind item that buyers will brag about for the next six months to all of their friends?

7) Where and to whom will you be selling your product/ service? Who are your suppliers? Who is your competition? What do you know about them?

8) How do you plan to produce this product/service? What raw materials will be used in the production process? What human resources will you need to draw on? What is your production cycle?

9) What price will you be selling your product/service for? What will the market bear? What must you sell it for to make a profit? What do comparable items sell for? Will this price cover your costs and provide ample profit?

10) What is your marketing strategy? How are you going to sell your product/service? How are you going to advertise? Will you hire a sales staff and/or use direct mail solicitation? What public relations efforts do you plan to incorporate?

11) Do you and/or your personnel have the necessary skills, qualifications and technical expertise to keep the business moving at a respectable clip and achieve the goals you've set forth?

12) What about your financial plans? How are you going to pay the costs of getting this business off the ground? Where is the money coming from to pay day-to-day expenses? As you grow and develop a track record you will be able to call on past performance to predict the future, but, with or without that track record, you need to know how you're going to handle financial needs and achieve a return on your investment.

You may have the answers to these questions already, but chances are you may find some holes in your thinking. In any case, the mere process of putting all of these elements in black and white can help you to focus. The act of preparing a plan forces you to recognize the weaknesses in your thinking and to identify the elements that you don't have clearly in place.

In the initial stages you don't need volumes of information in your business plan. Most of the critical questions can be answered in a sentence or a paragraph. The key is that the more precisely you can identify your answers, the closer you will be to success.

Your business plan will become your map to success, itemizing your ultimate goals for your business as well as the path you will follow to get there. It will also substantiate your loan-ability.

The basic business plan will get you moving and keep you focused. And, particularly during your first months of business ownership, it will keep you from getting sidetracked. As you become better grounded in your business plan and start using it day-to-day, you will begin to fine-tune it. Experience will show you the areas of your business that are shaky and where you need to focus your attention.

Typically, the marketing, management and financial areas of your business require constant adjustment. They are actually plans unto themselves. Each of these subplans is fluid, requiring regular adjustment if you hope to continue moving toward your goal. If you allow these elements to remain static, you will lose momentum. Following are overviews of each of these subplans. Later chapters cover these topics in much greater detail.

A Business Plan Outline

Business plans may take a variety of forms, but they must all contain information critical to lenders or investors. David Bangs, Jr. suggests the following outline:

Outline of a Business Plan

- Cover Sheet: Name of business, names of principals, address and phone number
- Statement of Purpose
- Table of Contents

Section One: The Business
   A. Description of Business
   B. Product/Service
   C. Market
   D. Location of Business
   E. Competition
   F. Management
   G. Personnel

H. Application and Expected Effect of Loan (if needed)

I. Summary

Section Two: Financial Data

A. Sources and Applications of Funding

B. Capital Equipment List

C. Balance Sheet

D. Break-Even Analysis

E. Income Projections (Profit and Loss Statements)
1. Three-year summary
2. Detail by month for first year
3. Detail by quarter for second and third years
4. Notes of explanation

F. Cash Flow Projection
1. Detail by month for first year
2. Detail by quarter for second and third years
3. Notes of explanation

G. Deviation Analysis

H. Historical Financial Reports for Existing Business
1. Balance sheets for past three years
2. Income statements for past three years
3. Tax returns

Section Three: Supporting Documents

Personal resumés, personal balance sheets, cost of living budget, credit reports, letters of reference, job descriptions, letters of intent, copies of leases, contracts, legal documents, and anything else relevant to the plan.

Source: Reprinted with permission from *The Business Planning Guide* by David H. Bangs, Jr., copyright 1992 by Upstart Publishing Company, Inc., 12 Portland St., Dover NH 03820 (800) 235-8866.

The Marketing Plan

This is where you show that there is a need for your product or service. Without a large enough need, no amount of management talent or financial backing can create a successful business. Marketing is the lifeblood of a business. Because of this, we have set aside a complete chapter to discuss it. No combination of marketing activities works all the time. Marketing requires a constant juggling of supply, resources and demand. Because your marketing mix will constantly change, you will need to adjust your efforts accordingly.

Your marketing plan is simply an expanded plan of action detailing how you will make your marketing strategy work, based on the priorities you have set for reaching your goals.

The marketing process is built on a firm foundation composed of the four Ps—*Product, Place* (distribution), *Price* and *Promotion*. Without all four elements nailed down and appropriately balanced, you do not have a marketing strategy—no matter how ambitious your promotional plans.

- *Product* What are you really selling?
- *Place* (distribution) How will you get that product to your customer?
- *Price* What is the right price (one acceptable to your customer and profitable to you)? Price your product or service too high, and you eliminate customers who can't afford you. Price your product too low, and you lose customers who think you don't offer something of quality because quality is often tied to price. Therefore, take the time to thoroughly research your market to find out what is being charged for the product or service you plan to sell.
- *Promotion* How will you promote your product or service? This category includes personal sales, advertising and public relations tools—promotional activities that stimulate interest, create desire and result in sales. Answer the customer's primary question, "What's in it for me?" by focusing on the unique benefits of the product/service and the customers' needs rather than features of the product or service.

In its broadest definition, marketing is the function of your business that includes all activities necessary to get your product/service in the hands of your customer. It requires market research, product development, pricing, packaging, advertising, transportation, sales and distribution and promotional activities including the use of public relations tools.

Because marketing can be a major business expense, marketing plans for the small business should, for the most part, incorporate more public relations efforts than any other form of marketing. Therefore, a large portion of our marketing chapter will address this effective strategy. Because there are so many different kinds of businesses, however, it is important that you take a look at a wide variety of strategies, using those that will be most effective for your particular business. Chapter 8 discusses in detail marketing for the small business.

The Management Plan

Perhaps a bit less formalized than the marketing plan and the financial plan, the management plan is important because it delineates how you will utilize the resources—physical, financial, and human—at your disposal to achieve your goals. If you don't take time to work through the details of day-to-day business operation, the business will rapidly get out of control. Guidelines, limitations and development stages need to be thought through and planned for carefully.

In management planning you will need to identify how, when, where and by whom the various functions of your business and office will be handled. You'll consider such mundane problems as furnishings and supplies, bookkeeping, billing and accounts receivable, taxes, office policies and procedures, and much more. It's a bit like preparing your car for a long trip. If you don't plan your gas, oil, tire and pit stop needs, you simply won't arrive at your destination.

The Financial Plan

The financial plan is critical to the success of your business plan. Despite the fact that it is usually developed for the benefit of potential lenders, keep in mind that such a plan is first and foremost important to *you*. Entrepreneurial businesses all too frequently straddle the financial edge, and you must have a firm grip on how financially sound you and your business are.

In your financial plan you will detail profits and losses, current assets and liabilities, budgets and the like. You will need to analyze your current financial health at a specific point in time and use your track record to project probable future growth.

Putting It All Together

Once you have done your homework—thoroughly researched, set your goals and expectations, planned your objectives and day-to-day operations, and determined all the key elements of your business—you will put that information into a formal document.

The first step is to assemble your working document. Some find that a three-ring binder with a separate page or section for each topic allows flexibility and ease of revision. If that works for you, fine. You will be reviewing your plan on a regular basis and updating it from time to time. For your own planning purposes, you will want to keep revisions as simple as possible.

But there will come a time when you will need to present this document to a lender, a consultant or others for review. That's when your communication and writing skills become extremely important.

Who is your audience? What do you expect to be the outcome of this document, and what information does the reader need to react in accordance with your expectations?

Before you write, prepare a reader-description list, as well as a list of key points that need to be addressed to support your cause. Answer readers' questions, leading them to the same conclusion that you addressed in the beginning of your document.

While you write, keep to the structure you have chosen. Make smooth transitional statements. Incorporate graphics and supporting documentation where needed. Close by repeating the main points of your opening remarks.

Now edit your plan. Consider asking someone with expertise in these matters to review it so that you can get a feel for any problems with your communication process. Your style and final presentation will follow basic business/technical writing techniques:

- *Watch the white space.* Make your presentation easy on the reader. Don't crowd your pages with details.

- *Use headings for each topic discussed.*   These will keep your presentation organized and will help the reader quickly locate information.
- *Keep your sentences short and concise.*   Eliminate editorial comments. Use active, descriptive nouns and verbs to convey your message.
- *Use transitional words and phrases throughout your report that help the reader follow your reasoning.*   For example, *now, because of this, so, additionally,* and other strong transitions show relationships and help your reader follow the logical flow of your work.
- *Precede all detailed object or process descriptions with an overview of function or purpose.*   Anticipate possible reader objections or questions, and incorporate explanations or answers into your plan.
- *Wherever you have supporting documentation, you might consider putting it in a separate appendix to keep your plan flowing.*
- *Make any limitations of your study clear from the beginning.*
- *Read over your writing twice.*   Read once for sense, and once for mechanical correctness; then ask someone else to read it.

Update Your Plan Regularly

Because you are in business to grow, and growth is predicated on change, you will need to review your plan on a regular basis. Your plan should be a working document—it's even wise to keep it handy for an occasional review, just to see if what you're doing is in keeping with your plans and goals.

Reevaluate every six months or at least every year. (Ideally, financial documents such as profit and loss statements and balance sheets should be updated monthly.) You will have to decide the best schedule for your business. Careful reevaluation is obviously indicated any time you are faced with major issues that may call for you to change direction. You may think you need to invest in a new computer or hire a manager. Don't do this without consulting your business plan. These are the kinds of steps that need to be evaluated in light of your overall plan.

You may reach a point where you discover that your marketing efforts aren't working—sales are off and you need to do something soon. This is definitely the time to check the marketing portion of your plan. Without these plans in place, you might decide too quickly that it's time to change your company image, or you may decide to change your marketing efforts drastically before they have had a chance to work. Your plan should help you to evaluate such issues in light of the bigger picture. View your planning documents as fluid; keep refining them, and they'll keep you growing.

Help in Preparing Your Plan

The small business development centers (SBDCs) located around the state offer help in the development of business plans (see Chapter 9). For example, at Elgin Community College's SBDC, future business owners receive a business plan workbook and guidance from a small business counselor. This center also offers entrepreneurs the opportunity to schedule a session at a computer facility where they can write their business plans using a special software program. This service is free to residents within the center's geographic boundaries.

Another resource is the Illinois Department of Commerce and Community Affairs (DCCA), which offers a sample business plan in its *One Stop Business Start-Up Kit* described in Chapter 2. Five plans are available for different types of businesses. Call the Illinois Small Business Hotline at (800) 252-2923 to order the kit and obtain the name of the SBDC nearest you.

Business plan kits are also available from Commerce Clearing House in Chicago. They offer the *How To Write Your Own Business Plan Project Kit* for $85, *How To Write Your Business Plan* Software Package for $125 and a video called *How To Write a Business Plan* for $49.95. Call (312) 346-9134 to order.

Publications

The SBA offers a wide variety of booklets on topics of interest to those who manage small businesses. Some of the titles are listed here, but call 800-U-ASK-SBA to request the most recent edition of the SBA *Directory of Business Development Publications.*

> *The Business Plan for Homebased Businesses* If you are convinced that a profitable home business is attainable, this publication will provide a step-by-step guide to develop a plan.

Business Plan for Retailers   Learn how to develop a business plan for a retail business.

Business Plan for Small Construction Firms   This publication is designed to help an owner/manager of a small construction company pull together the resources to develop a business plan.

Business Plan for Small Manufacturers   Designed to help an owner/manager of a small manufacturing firm, this publication covers all the basic information necessary to develop an effective business plan.

Business Plan for Small Service Firms   An outline of the key points to be included in a small service firm's business plan.

Checklist for Going into Business   This best seller highlights important considerations you should know when deciding whether or not to start your business.

Developing a Strategic Business Plan   A guide to developing a strategic action plan for your small business.

Planning and Goal Setting for Small Businesses   Learn how to plan for success.

Abrams, Rhonda M., *The Successful Business Plan: Secrets & Strategies*. Oasis Press, 1991.

Bangs, David H. Jr., *The Business Planning Guide: Creating a Plan for Success in Your Business*. Upstart Publishing Co., 1992. Also by the same author and publisher, *The Market Planning Guide, The Cash Flow Control Guide* and *The Personnel Planning Guide*.

Brooks, Julie K. and Barry A. Stevens, *How To Write a Successful Business Plan*. American Management Association, (AMA), 1986.

Buskirk, Richard H., Courtney Price and R. Mack Davis, *The Entrepreneur's Planning Handbook*. Creative Management Unlimited, Inc., 1987.

Delaney, Robert Jr. and Robert Howell, *How To Prepare an Effective Business Plan: A Step-By-Step Approach*. American Management Association, 1986.

Hosmer, LaRue T. and Roger Guiles, *Creating the Successful Business Plan*. Oasis Press, 1987.

How To Create a Winning Business Plan. Caddylac Systems, 1987.

How To Develop a Successful Business Plan. Entrepreneur Magazine/American Entrepreneur Institute, 1985.

Mancuso, Joseph R., *How To Write a Winning Business Plan*. Prentice Hall, 1990.

McKeever, Mike, *Start-:Up Money: How To Write a Business Plan*. Nolo Press, 1989.

Rich, Stanley R. and David Gumbert, *Business Plans That Win $$$: Lessons from the MIT Enterprise Forum*. HarperCollins Inc., 1987.

Siegal, Eric S., Loren A. Schultz and Brian R. Ford, *The Arthur Young Business Plan Guide*. John Wiley & Sons, 1991.

Software Programs

Today, many business tasks are automated, and business plan writing is no exception. One of the best programs is *BizPlan Builder Tools for Sales*, which provides you with an actual template of a business plan. You access files through either your word processor or a spreadsheet program, and then fill in the blanks with the information you have gathered. When you are finished, you have created your business plan. This program is particularly beneficial for those who have difficulty writing, and can significantly reduce the time it takes to construct a plan. It is, however, necessary to do the research behind the information and numbers you plug in. Call (415) 941-9191 or (800) 346-5426 to order.

Another good program is *Success, Inc.*, a Dynamic Pathways Program; call (714) 720-8462 to order. Unlike *BizPlan Builder*, *Success* is an interactive software package that has a series of questions for you to answer. The program then creates a printed business plan from your answers.

A relative newcomer to the business plan software market is *PFS: Business Plan for Windows* by Spinnaker Software Corp, (617) 494-1200. The program has all of the regular portions of a business plan with the additional capability of producing graphs to visually support the results of your research and projections.

Consultants

An average business plan can take more than 200 hours to write. Hiring someone who knows the process and what it looks like—especially if you are putting a substantial amount of money into your business—becomes a strong consideration. The difference between doing it yourself or taking a course in college is the critical perspective. Jill Johnson comments on the role a management consultant takes in the business plan process:

A consultant who works with you to develop a business plan will work with you on the research or do the research for you, interpret the information as it relates to you and what you want to achieve. The consultant will give you objective feedback as to how your ideas fit within your marketplace and help you understand how they fit your operating issues, staffing issues and the total financial impact they will have. Some consultants will also act as a guide, helping you develop your own successful plan.

Your business plan must be realistic. You need to take an active role in its development even if you are using consultants to help you. The time spent creating a realistic, workable plan will have a substantial payback as you grow your business.

■ Seven ■

Financing Sources

■

    Financing is one of the toughest areas for an entrepreneur to address. During the current recession, drastic cutbacks have taken their toll on a number of financial institutions. There are no simple tricks or shortcuts to getting money—only old-fashioned strategies that often aren't taken seriously enough.

    Don't accept quick and easy solutions. Look at the process from all angles before making any decisions. Be sure that you understand cash flow analysis and financial planning well enough to at least ask the right questions—before making any decisions.

    This chapter provides an overview of the funding resources available to both the start-up and emerging business. However, the existing business is likely to meet with more success in obtaining financing. Our advice is to use the resources as a starting point to begin seeking funding. Prepare yourself for the process by setting aside blocks of time for researching, planning, writing and meeting potential funding sources. You will find that looking for funding becomes, at the very least, a part-time job.

    Try to seek loans for growth rather than for working capital. First, look for loans at your current bank. The relationship you have been developing for the past start-up years should serve as a foundation for lending. Following is a loan package checklist. Use it to complete the documents you will be required to present for most loan requests.

Once you have developed a financial track record—usually after two or three years in business—you become eligible for a much broader range of funding opportunities. Both the state and federal governments have a variety of funding programs. You will need to meet certain financial qualifications, such as adequate collateral and increased annual revenues. If you have shown financial success, you are in a good position to request funding for expansion. Funding sources are often reluctant to lend for operating expenses. They want to see the funds they lend being used to develop new business opportunities.

Loan Package Checklist

Your accountant and banker can be valuable resources in helping you construct the financial section of your loan package—the first step toward obtaining financing. Your financial profile is critical in substantiating your loan-ability. Listed below are the basics of a loan request:

General statement regarding the Loan Request

- Purpose—What exactly will the loan be used for?
- Loan amount
- Repayment terms

Definition of Product/Service Sold

- Description of product/service
- Strength/weakness of product/service sales strategy
- Who is your potential market? Supporting demographics
- How product is/will be sold
- Trade area/competition
- Sales volumes—historical/projected

Place of Business

- Location
- Description of physical facility/equipment/inventory

Resumé of Owner/Principals/Management—What are your specific strengths?

Financial Information (three years minimum, if available)

- Company Balance Sheet
- Company Profit & Loss Statement
- Company Federal Tax Returns
- Company Pro Forma Statements (minimum two-year forecast)
- Personal Financial Statements on all principals
- Personal Tax Returns on all principals

Ratios That Indicate Loan-Ability

Your lender will be interested in financial ratios when evaluating your loan request. Below is an explanation of three key ratios.

Current Ratio—This indicates the strength of the company in servicing additional debt. A 2:1 ratio allows a reasonable margin of safety:

$$\frac{\text{Current Assets}}{\text{Current Liabilities}}$$

Current Assets = cash, accounts receivable, short-term investments
Current Liabilities = accounts payable, interest accrued, etc.

Acid Test Ratio This indicates whether the company can meet its current debt obligations. A ratio of 1:1 or higher is satisfactory

$$\frac{\text{Liquid (Quick) Assets}}{\text{Current Liabilities}}$$

Liquid Assets = cash and investments that can easily be converted to cash
Current Liabilities = accounts payable, interest accrued, etc.

Ownership Ratio This indicates what you have at stake in the business

$$\frac{\text{Liabilities}}{\text{Net Worth}}$$

Liabilities = monies owed by the business
Net Worth = amount of owner's equity or money at stake

Types of Loans

- *Character*   After you have built up a history with a bank, an uninsured loan that is basically based on your character may be considered.
- *Lines of Credit*   This involves loans for financing a short-term asset. A line of credit is drawn upon either seasonally or during a specific time in the cash flow cycle of a business. This draw is usually paid off during another time in that same cash flow cycle. The rate on a line of credit is usually floating with prime so that it is adjusted by the market. The term of a line of credit is never more than 12 months; however, lines are renewed yearly with updated financial information. These loans are typically referred to as *working capital loans*.
- *Term Loans (i.e., one-year, five-year, fifteen-year)*   Term loans often require collateral and high credit standards. They are usually installment loans that blend the interest and principal into monthly or quarterly payments.
- *Co-signer Loans*   These loans are most typically used in the consumer finance or retail banking industries. The co-signer is one who personally guarantees the performance of the borrower on the loan. Typically the borrower has little or no credit experience, while the co-signer has a significant amount of good credit experience.
- *Warehouse (Field Warehouse) Loans*   Commonly known as "Warehouse lines of credit," these loans are associated with brokerage businesses. A mortgage loan broker uses the line to fund a loan underwritten to the specifications of a particular securities pool. The line is advanced for a short-term and may then be readvanced numerous times as the preceeding loans are funded and then sold as a security.
- *Equipment Loan/Installment* (usually directed at manufacturing companies)   Your equipment is the collateral for this type of loan.
- *Accounts Receivable Financing*   In the commercial banking business receivables are used strictly as collateral. Typically a commercial bank will advance a line that is a percentage of the business receivables. Some commercial credit companies will finance a percentage of receivables; however, such

loans are usually at very high interest rates.

- *Trade Credit* These loans are made between two or more businesses. Technically trade credits are an accounts payable that is owed to a supplier and used to purchase inventory. That supplier may offer a trade discount to the purchaser. A discount—two percent/ten days—means that if the supplier gets paid in ten days, the purchaser gets a discount of two percent. This type of lending is secured by the product and is a nonbanking type of financing.

Strategies for Securing a Business Loan

For those who think their businesses would be successful *if* only they had an infusion of capital, here are the strategies that can boost your chances for success:

Create an Excellent Business Plan

See Chapter 6. All funding sources will want to see a comprehensive, concise and realistic business plan. Your plan will be the primary key for getting funding and, if used as a basis for daily business decisions, will help you reach your goals and give you continued opportunities for funding.

Start a File on Contacts

Whether you have a computerized data base or keep a notebook of the many contacts you make with potential investors, it's important to keep track. Once you have completed your business plan, mail it with a cover letter to the investors you have prescreened. Prescreening is important because you should not waste money copying or mailing to unscreened individuals. Take the time to make phone calls, and see if at this time (because things change constantly with every business), the bank, angel network, venture capital firm, etc., is accepting applications for your type of investment request. Time taken to target market is the best time you can spend.

Continue to Periodically Follow Up on Your Contacts

"If at first you don't succeed, try, try again," is an excellent motto when applying for funding. Just as you must constantly sell your product or service, you must sell the opportunity to others to invest in your company. Make regular phone follow-ups (monthly or every other month) even to contacts who were noncommittal or negative. Your initial negative contact with a representative of a bank or investment firm might have involved just a bad day for the person with whom you had spoken. As long as there was an initial interest in your company, keep trying. Ask for suggestions on how to improve your plan. The advice you get could mean the difference between just wishing for an opportunity and making one happen.

Ask for a Larger Sum of Money Than You Need

Many entrepreneurs make the mistake of not asking for enough money. Banks, investors and even the SBA see this as a sign that you don't have a good understanding of what your needs are. Keep in mind that your success in obtaining funding really hinges on your preparation. Take the time to seek advice from professionals. Some banks even offer to help you create realistic financial projections at no cost. SBDCs can also assist you. Take your projections to your accountant, or seek the assistance of an accountant who has worked with companies like yours. This extra preparation may not ensure that you will get funding, but your clear, unshakable understanding of your business's financial health, it's potential for growth and the value of money will go a long way toward convincing your lenders to invest in you.

Lenders no longer—if they ever did—buy the concept of "blue sky." Money is spent on a realistic, projected return on investment now more than ever before. The key, if you want to become financially strong and if you want to secure funding, is to become money wise in every sense of the word.

Financial Resource #1—The SBA

A good place to begin your education on financial matters is the SBA, which publishes a variety of booklets on all relative subjects. Call the Illinois Business Hotline at (800) 252-2923 for a current *SBA Directory of Business Development Publications* that will include the following:

ABC's of Borrowing   Some small business people cannot understand why a lending institution would refuse to lend them money. Others have no trouble getting funds but are surprised to find strings attached to their loans. Learn the fundamentals of borrowing.

Accounting Services for Small Service Firms Sample profit/loss statements are used to illustrate how accounting services can help expose and correct trouble spots in a business's financial records.

Analyze Your Records To Reduce Costs Cost reduction is not simply slashing any and all expenses. Understand the nature of expenses and how they interrelate with sales, inventories and profits. Achieve greater profits through more efficient use of the dollar.

Basic Budgets for Profit Planning This publication takes the worry out of putting together a comprehensive budgeting system to monitor your profits and assess your financial operations.

Budgeting in a Small Service Firm Learn how to set up and keep sound financial records. Study how to effectively use journals, ledgers and charts to increase profits.

A Pricing Checklist for Small Retailers The owner/manager of a small real estate business can use this checklist to apply proven pricing strategies that can lead to profits.

Pricing Your Products and Services Profitably Read this to learn how to price your products profitably, how to use the various techniques of pricing and when to use these techniques to your advantage.

Profit Costing and Pricing for Manufacturers Uncover the latest techniques for pricing your products profitably.

Record-keeping in a Small Business A description of how to set up a useful record-keeping system.

Simple Breakeven Analysis for Small Stores Learn how "breakeven analysis" enables the manager/owner to make better decisions concerning sales, profits and costs.

Sound Cash Management and Borrowing Avoid a "cash crisis" through proper use of cash budgets, cash flow projections and planned borrowing concepts.

Understanding Cash Flow To survive, a business must have enough cash to meet its obligations. This book shows you how to plan for the movement of cash through your business and thus plan for future requirements.

A Venture Capital Primer for Small Business This best seller highlights the venture capital resources available and how to develop a proposal for obtaining these funds.

For the most part, the SBA will not make direct loans, but it will support a small business with an SBA guaranteed loan made through a bank. Be aware that the SBA will not finance or guarantee loans for real estate, speculation or creative services such as writers, printers, artists or musicians.

■ Resource

Name of Resource:	Small Business Administration—Region V Office
Where To Find It:	Northwest Atrium 500 W. Madison, Ste. 1250 Chicago, IL 60661-2511 (312) 353-4578
Who Could Use It:	Recommended for those who are able to commit 30 percent of the monies requested as a down payment
What It Contains:	Assistance with directing you to lenders (See list of certified/preferred lenders below.)
Why Use It:	Possible financing for those who might not be able to obtain conventional loans.
When To Use It:	When you have the prerequisite financial profile (call for details)
What You Need To Get an SBA Loan:	<ul><li>At least 30 percent collateral for the loan request</li><li>Substantial expertise in the business you are entering</li><li>A solid business plan</li><li>A personal guarantee that the money will be repaid by you if you default on the loan</li><li>A bank that will serve as the lender</li></ul> According to the SBA, an applicant will not be turned down because of a shortage of collateral alone. This is not as important as repayment ability.

Certified/Preferred SBA Lenders in Illinois

For an updated list of certified/preferred SBA lenders, contact the SBA's Washington, DC Office of Financial Institutions (312) 353-4528.

Certified lender lists are updated every two years. According to the SBA there has been an increase in the number of people applying for loans as well as in the number of approvals—approximately 30 percent more activity than there was two years ago. The following list of preferred Illinois lenders was updated in 1992.

Albany Bank & Trust Co., N.A. (PLP)
3400 W. Lawrence
Chicago, IL 60625
(312) 267-7300

Bank of Bellwood
219 S. Mannheim Rd.
Bellwood, IL 60104
(708) 547-3650

Bank One
E. Old State Capital Plaza
Springfield, IL 62701
(217) 525-9600

Bank One Champaign
201 W. University
Champaign, IL 61820
(217) 351-1600

Boatmen's National Bank of Belleville
23 Public Square
Belleville, IL 62222
(618) 233-6600

Busey First National Bank (PLP)
201 W. Main
Urbana, IL 61801
(217) 384-4500

Colonial Bank
5850 W. Belmont
Chicago, IL 60634-5299
(312) 283-3700

Edens Bank
3245 Lake Ave.
Wilmette, IL 60091
(708) 256-5105

Firstar Naper Bank
136 S. Washington
Naperville, IL 60566
(708) 983-8800

First National Bank & Trust Co.
401 E. State St.
PO Box 4900
Rockford, IL 61110-4900
(815) 962-3771

ITT Small Business Finance Corp.
9730 S. Western, Ste. 335
Evergreen Park, IL 60642
(708) 857-8488

ITT Small Business Finance Corp.
2055 Craigshire Rd., Ste. 400
St. Louis, MO 63146
(314) 576-0872

The Money Store
1901 N. Roselle Rd., Ste. 800
Schaumburg, IL 60195
(708) 490-6433

Seaway National Bank of Chicago
645 E. 87th St.
Chicago, IL 60619
(312) 487-4800

South Central Bank & Trust
555 W. Roosevelt Rd.
Chicago, IL 60607
(312) 421-7100

The South Shore Bank of Chicago
7054 S. Jeffrey Ave.
Chicago, IL 60649
(312) 288-1000

Union National Bank & Trust Company
1 Fountain Square Plaza
Elgin, IL 60120
(708) 888-7500

United IL Bank of Benton (PLP)
701 Public Square, Box 790
Benton, IL 62812
(618) 439-4381

Other SBA Resources

Government Assistance Almanac
Omnigraphics, Inc.
Penobscot Building
Detroit, MI 48226 or call (800) 234-1340

A guide to federal financial and other domestic assistance programs that offers information on loans, grants, insurance, personal payments and benefits, fellowships, subsidies, scholarships, traineeships, technical information, advisory services, investigation of complaints, and sales and donations of federal property. The almanac also provides comparative tables on funding for the last four fiscal years, with the 50 largest and 50 smallest programs for the year 1990 highlighted.

How To Raise Money for a Small Business
Office of Business Development & Marketing
U.S. Small Business Administration
409 Third St. S.W.
Washington, DC 20416
202-205-6665

A free fact sheet from the government that outlines the basics for raising money. It also contains information on how to write a loan proposal. SBA programs and descriptions of each are listed on the sheet.

The Small Business Guide to Federal Research and Development Funding Opportunities
Office of Small Business Research and Development
National Science Foundation
(202) 653-5202

A free guide to federal research and development programs in the various United States governmental agencies.

Financial Resource #2—The Illinois Department of Commerce and Community Affairs (DCCA)

According to DCCA's most recent handbook, *Development Financing Program*, "Funds for most business assistance programs are limited. Only the most competitive applications are funded. Additionally, participation in many of these programs is dependent on the creation and retention of jobs."

As with SBA loans, state loans are primarily for existing businesses. However, a few loans are earmarked for start-ups:

Illinois Department of Commerce and Community Affairs
100 W. Randolph, Ste. 3-400
Chicago, IL 60601
(312) 814-7179
or call
the Illinois Business Hotline
(800) 252-2923

Limited funding programs are available. A good resource for companies that have completed business and marketing plans, experienced management and are minority/female-owned firms that have experienced difficultiy raising venture capital. To obtain a copy of *Development Financing Programs*, call the numbers listed above.

Women's Finance Initiative
Illinois Treasurer's Office
State of Illinois Center, Ste. 15-600
Chicago, IL 60601
(312) 814-3571

Business loans of up to $50,000 are available for qualified women-owned businesses one to three years old; loans of more than $50,000 are available to qualified women-owned businesses with a track record of more than three years.

Low-interest loans are available for qualified businesses at least one year old. The Initiative is a partnership that offers women business owners the following resources:

- An Illinois Treasurer's list of banks that provide financing
- Business development groups that help target services where they are needed most and make sure women have the information they need to take advantage of the Initiative.
- Financial institutions that offer low-interest loans to strengthen emerging businesses and to expand those that are already off to a promising start

Financial Resource #3—SBICs and MESBICs

SBICs (Small Business Investment Companies) licensed by SBA, have come into existence as a result of the 1958 *Small Business Investment Act*. Their purpose is to make equity funding and long-term credit available *only to small business*. If you have no incorporation plans, you may qualify for long-term loans— more than five years—secured by real estate or other collateral . If you are incorporated, you may be eligible for long-term or equity loans that allow for sale of stock, attached or convertible debentures or loans with stock-purchase warrants. MESBICs (Minority Enterprise Small Business Investment Companies) are licensed by the federal government and may receive some funds from the SBA. Both SBICs and MESBICs are privately organized and managed companies.

There are approximately 360 SBICs in the United States. They are a major source of money, offering investments ranging from an average of $60,000 to as much as $3 million. These lenders, who often take greater risks than banks, offer management skills and experience. They are federally licensed and performance reviewed by the SBA, ensuring fair and honest treatment.

SBICs are not the best source for small (a few thousand dollars) loans. Be forewarned that your profit potential may not be sufficient to attract their interest. SBICs are licensed by the SBA, and many prefer equity positions (partnership interests).

Their loans are long-term—five years or more. Below are some local and national resources:

Alpha Capital Venture Partners LP
Three First National Plaza, Ste. 1400
Chicago, IL 60602
(312) 214-3440

This small business investment corporation provides venture capital and has no industry preference; however, no real estate, oil and gas, or start-up venture is considered. All investments are structured to provide equity participation in the business—no straight loans are considered. Their minimum investment is $200,000; preferred size of investment is $500,000 to $1 million. The funded company must be located in the Midwest.

National Association of Investment Companies
1111 14th St. N.W., Ste. 700
Washington, DC 20005
(202) 289-4336

For a minimal cost, this association provides a directory of over 150 venture capital firms specializing in the minority sector.

National Association of Small Business Investment Companies
1199 N. Fairfax St., Ste. 200
Alexandria, VA 22314
(703) 683-1601

This trade association for small business investment companies offers sources of start-up and operating capital. A free directory of members is available.

Business Ventures, Inc.
20 N. Wacker Dr., Ste. 1741
Chicago, IL 60606
(312) 346-1580

A small business investment corporation which, although it has no industry preference, considers only ventures in the Chicago area. (For older businesses.)

Continental Illinois Venture Corp. (CIVC)
231 S. LaSalle St.
Chicago, IL 60697
(312) 828-8021

A small business investment corporation that provides start-up and early-stage financing to growth-oriented companies with

capable management teams, proprietary products and expanding markets.

Financial Resource #4—Venture Capital and Private Investment Firms

For the most part, venture capital firms will not consider
start-ups. Venture capital funding, the most expensive of funding resources, usually looks for at least a 20 percent equity
position in a company and often a share of more than 50 percent.
Most entrepreneurs consider this funding as an alternative only
after they have exhausted the possibility of self-financing.

However, there are businesses, such as high technology
companies, that need a great deal of money to position themselves quickly and effectively in market niches. When time is of
the essence and the business has a diverse team of seasoned
professionals coming together to build a business, venture capital might be just the right form of financing.

Venture capital is one of the more appropriate resources for
a *second-round* investment in a company in order to ensure its
continued expansion. The company, initially funded with the
owner's finances, has grown to the point where it clearly demon-
strates success and a growth curve that shows a reasonable
chance of creating an open-ended market. By the time the company needs a second round of financing, the niche should be
clearly defined. Again, a business plan is required with sound
projections based on a two-year to five-year financial track record.

It could take up to a year or more to get funding once a firm
is interested in your proposal. Venture firms receive 100 or more
funding proposals *weekly*. Most firms have a board that reviews
applicants. If they are interested in you, they can continue to
request new information and hold meetings until they are ready
to make a decision.

Venture capitalists prefer businesses that are novel and interesting enough to promise a fairly short-term buy-out, an opportunity to go public and high profit returns. They like to consider
businesses with fairly sophisticated original investors oriented
toward long-term investments who intend to reinvest on the
second round. Venture capitalists usually want more than a 20
percent ownership interest in the business in exchange for certain

investment monies. The younger the business, the higher the equity interest requested. Along with this interest comes management support and expertise that may be beneficial.

But be aware that only an elite few will ever successfully woo a venture capitalist.

Typically venture capitalists look for:

- A track record and a good reputation in your industry as well as in-depth, relevant experience. Often a minimum of ten years in management and five years in a position of significant responsibility are required.
- The potential for enormous growth is necessary—usually $50-$100 million in revenues. Venture capitalists typically look for companies that will require at least $1 million.
- A strong management team is preferred over an individual.
- A concise business plan is required of at least 10 but not more than 25 pages including a summary of financial information for which there's a lot of back-up and an Executive Summary—a two-page overview of your business, your market, your request for financing and your estimated explanation of when and how you will buy back the equity interest. This should also include answers to why this business makes sense from a competitive standpoint and what the target market will be.
- Essential qualities of the company that must be outlined when seeking to attract venture capitalists, include:
  - ability to evaluate and react to risk well;
  - leadership demonstrated in the past;
  - at least ten times return in five to ten years;
  - a thorough familiarity with the market and the capacity for sustained intense effort.

Network with lawyers and accountants who do a significant amount of venture activity as intermediaries to venture capitalists. Or, try a venture-capital club meeting where entrepreneurs can pitch their ideas to a room full of venture capitalists and private investors. (See International Venture Capital Institute on the next page.)

Research carefully before applying. Find out how much the venture capitalists' minimum investment is, what sort of companies they like to back, how much they've invested in the past year and who some of their big winners are. Be confident, assured and, most of all, prepared—for either success or rejection.

■ Resources _____

Resources for Locating Venture Capital Suppliers

Name of Resource: *Crain's Chicago Business* (February issue)

Where To Find It: 740 N. Rush St.
Chicago, IL 60611-9791
(312) 588-1313

What It Contains: *Crain's* publishes a yearly list of venture capital firms and states that although money is tight, there are firms that have increased their investment monies. The majority of the investments are with high technology companies; however, there are companies available for almost every type of investment imaginable.

Name of Resource: International Venture Capital Institute, Inc.

Where To Find It: PO Box 1333
Stamford, CT 06904
(203) 323-3143

What It Contains: Directory lists 100 United States and 15 foreign clubs

Why Use It: To obtain a comprehensive list of venture capital companies

Name of Resource: National Venture Capital Association

Where To Find It: 1655 N. Fort Myer Dr., Ste. 700
Arlington, VA 22209
(703) 528-4370

Who Could Use It: Any business

What It Contains: A professional association for the venture-capital industry with more than 235 member firms. A membership directory is available to small businesses.

Why Use It: To obtain a listing of firms

Name of Resource: Nebraska Business Development Center

Where To Find It: 1313 Farnam St., Ste. 132
Omaha, NE 68182
(402) 595-2381

Who Could Use It:	Any business
What It Contains:	A free list of more than 60 venture capital clubs—send $ .45 for handling and a #10 envelope.
Why Use It:	To obtain a listing of venture firms
Name of Resource:	International Venture Capital Institute, Inc.
Where To Find It:	PO Box 1333
	Stamford, CT 06904
	(203) 323-3143
Who Could Use It:	Those considering international expansion
What It Contains:	Directory lists 100 United States and 15 foreign clubs

Venture Capital for the Start-Up

Name of Resource:	Basic Search, Inc.
Where To Find It:	Park Place
	10 W. Streetsboro St.
	Hudson, OH 44236
	(216) 656-2442 Monday through Friday, 9:00 A.M.-1:30 P.M.
Who Could Use It:	Any business owner
What It Contains:	This is one of the few venture capitalists that offers financial assistance to start-ups.
Name of Resource:	The Capital Strategy Group, Inc.
Where To Find It:	20 N. Wacker Dr.
	Chicago, IL 60606
	(312) 444-1170
Who Could Use It:	Any business in manufacturing or service industries
What It Contains:	This investment banker/venture capital supplier provides financing to start-up and early-stage manufacturing or service industry companies, located in the Midwest.
Name of Resource:	Capital Health Management
Where To Find It:	122 S. Michigan, Ste. 1915
	Chicago, IL 60603
	(312) 427-1227
Who Could Use It:	Early-stage (start-up or research process ready to produce something) health care and medical technology businesses

What It Contains:	Private, corporate and institutional monies are available for financing. Submit a business plan. (They receive 100 to 200 business plans a year.) All requests are responded to in approximately four to six weeks. If there is interest in your business, the process could run approximately six months to a year.

Name of Resource:	Cerulean Fund
Where To Find It:	1701 E. Lake Ave., Ste. 275 Glenview, IL 60025 (708) 657-8002
Who Could Use It:	Diversified
What It Contains:	This group of institutions and individuals is interested in investing in early-stage companies generating at least $1 million in sales annually. However, companies generating less also will be reviewed.
Why Use It:	Seed capital—$25,000-$500,000

Name of Resource:	Continental Illinois Venture Corp. (CIVC)
Where To Find It:	231 S. LaSalle St. Chicago, IL 60697 (312) 828-8021
Who Could Use It:	Any business
What It Contains:	This small business investment corporation provides start-up and early-stage financing to growth-oriented companies with capable management teams, proprietary products and expanding markets.

Venture Capital Suppliers for the Growing Business

Note: Some of the resources listed below consider funding for both start-up and growing businesses. Check the heading "What it Contains" for this information.

Name of Resource:	Allstate Venture Capital
Where To Find It:	Allstate Plaza, South Bldg. G5D Northbrook, IL 60062 (708) 402-5681
Who Could Use It:	Any business

What It Contains: This venture capital supplier does not limit investments to particular industries or geographical locations. Interest is in unique products or services that address large potential markets and offer great economic benefits; strength of management team is also important. Investments range from $500,000 to $5 million.

Name of Resource: Ameritech Development Corp.
Where To Find It: Ten S. Wacker Dr., 21st Fl.
Chicago, IL 60606
(312) 609-6000
Who Could Use It: High-tech companies
What It Contains: This venture capital supplier seeks ideas in high-technology information management that relate to Ameritech's existing business in telecommunications technologies.

Name of Resource: Chicago Capital Fund
Where To Find It: 208 S. LaSalle St., Ste. 1154
Chicago, IL 60604
(312) 855-6050
Who Could Use It: In order to be considered, companies have to be headquartered and have 75 percent of their operations and employment in Chicago.
What It Contains: Subordinated debt (uncollaterized) and equity. Funding comes from private and corporate investors. Equity positions would start at 20 percent ownership of the company. Looking for companies generating yearly revenues of at least $1 million.

Name of Resource: Eager Enterprises, Inc.
Where To Find It: 640 N. LaSalle St., Ste. 560
Chicago, IL 60610
(312) 642-7560
What It Contains: Eager provides funding (that comes from institutional and individual investors) for companies developing information services and transaction processing.

Name of Resource: Frontenac Co.
Where To Find It: 208 S. LaSalle St., Ste. 1900
                          Chicago, IL 60604
                          (312) 368-0044
What It Contains: Pension funds, institutions, partners' capital

Name of Resource: IEG Venture Management, Inc.
Where To Find It: Ten Riverside Plaza
                          Chicago, IL 60606
                          (312) 644-0890
What It Contains: This venture capital supplier provides start-up financing primarily to companies in the Midwest that focus on productivity-enhancing technologies in the medical, manufacturing, electronic, telecommunications, agricultural, service, chemical and mineral, and metal products industries.

Name of Resource: Seidman Jackson Fisher and Co.
Where To Find It: 233 N. Michigan Ave., Ste. 1812
                          Chicago, IL 60601
                          (312) 856-1812
Who Could Use It: Limited market; see below
What It Contains: This private venture capital supplier provides early-stage and growth-equity financing to companies with proprietary patented products or services that deal with large and rapidly growing industrial markets. There is a limited interest in consumer markets. Leveraged buy outs are considered under certain circumstances. Investments range from $200,000 to $2 million.

Venture Capital for Women Entrepreneurs

Name of Resource: National Association for Female Executives (NAFE) Venture Capital Program
Where To Find It: 127 W. 24 St.
                          New York, NY 10011
                          (212) 645-0770
Who Could Use It: Any female-owned business—start-up or existing enterprise. All principals of the company must be women.

What It Contains:	This fund has access to as much as $50,000 in venture capital. Eligibility requirements are: you must be an NAFE member (annual dues are $29), and you must submit a traditional business plan including information on the amount you would like the NAFE Venture Capital Program to invest.

Financial Resource #5—Angel Networks

Angels are private individuals with money who are often interested in participating in the companies they invest in. Unlike most venture capital firms, these investors are interested in obtaining a smaller share of your company's equity in exchange for their knowledge, experience and of course, dollars. How do you locate an angel? One way is through angel networks. Where venture capital firms provide $1 billion yearly in seed monies for businesses, more than $27 billion is spent by angels. Most of these investors are successful entrepreneurs who are looking to invest in younger companies. There are roughly 20 angel networks around the country. Following is a list of resources that can help you locate angels:

■ Resources

Name of Resource:	MIT Enterprise Forum
Where To Find It:	201 Vassar St.
	Cambridge, MA 02139
	617-253-8240
Who Could Use It:	Any business
What It Contains:	For a $250 fee you will be listed in the data base and will receive a list of angel networks. This network produces a monthly newsletter for registered participants, which provides general tips for fund seekers and information on projects being funded.
Name of Resource:	Seed Capital Network, Inc.
Where To Find It:	8905 Kingston Pike, Ste. 12
	Knoxville, TN 37923
	(615) 573-4655

What It Contains:	A three-month membership in the network costs $250. This private sector company, with 600 members in the United States, introduces entrepreneurs to wealthy, private individuals who belong to the network's client-investor pool. Seed Capital provides a computer-based screening service that makes fast, confidential linkups between entrepreneurs and investors. Investments range from $5,000-$950,000.
Who Could Use It:	Companies at any stage of development including start-up
When To Use It:	For start-ups and beyond

Funding for Social Ventures

There is a special investor network available to emerging businesses that provide social benefits to others.

Name of Resource:	Social Venture Investor Briefings A Project of the Investors' Circle
Where To Find It:	156 Whittington Course St. Charles, IL 60174 (708) 513-8384
What It Contains:	Call to request information about the briefings and directions for preparing a two-page summary. For a fee of approximately $150, your completed summary is circulated and investors interested in your company will contact you directly.
Who Could Use It:	This company works with companies in all development stages that are socially responsible. Key areas of interest for investors include: energy reduction, environmental issues, poverty reduction, sustainable forestry, education, infant development, women's economic development, minority enterprise, preventive health, corporate and institutional responsibility, international peace, media and domestic and international development, etc.

Research for Financing Opportunities

Financing is your most important consideration, and there is quite a bit of information available. Visit your bookstore or library to see some of the literature available on financing. You might also research in small business magazines, since financing is a common subject for articles.

As Bruce Biechman and Jay Conrad Levinson so concisely say in their book *Guerrilla Financing, Alternative Techniques to Finance Any Small Business*, "Yes, guerrillas, there *is* a way to finance your business. Don't think for one moment that there is a lack of capital out there. It is not lack of capital that stops most people. It is the lack of information on how to *get* that capital." Information gathering is always the starting point in developing your own business strategies.

This chapter is just a starting point. Constantly be on the lookout for new sources and creative ways to obtain funding. You are not alone. Most business start-ups—even many famous ones like Nike, Ben and Jerry's Ice Cream, and Borland Software—had little initial capital. Yet they grew financially healthy by constantly learning, seeking out and building a wealth of information on their market. As Jenny Craig once said, "Success happens when preparation meets opportunity."

Be prepared. Seek out new opportunities through books, personal contacts, special interest groups and professional development courses. Work from a position of strength. As many business bankers will tell you, it's better to look for money when you don't need it.

And now, a few more recommendations:

■ Resources _____

Name of Resource:	American Women's Economic Development Corp. (AWED)
Where To Find It:	641 Lexington Ave., 9th Fl. New York, NY 10022 (800) 222-AWED (2933) or (212) 688-1900
Who Could Use It:	Female business owners
What It Contains:	A nonprofit organization that provides

management training and business counseling for start-up and expanding female-
owned businesses.

Name of Resource:	*Small Business Resource Guide*
Where To Find It:	The National Association for the Self-Em-ployed
	Commonwealth Plaza
	PO Box 612067
	DFW Airport, TX 75261
	(800) 232-NASE
What It Contains:	This comprehensive overview of the fi-nancing process and of lenders includes samples of loan packages required in vari-ous situations and lists of local and na-tional lending institutions.
Why Use It:	To gain a better understanding of the vari-ety of loans available to businesses; what is required to obtain them; and who makes them. Also this will help you identify the specific most appropriate lenders.

-- ■

Publications

Biechman, Bruce and Jay Conrad Levinson, *Guerrilla Financing, Alternative Techniques To Finance Any Small Business.* Houghton Mifflin
Company, 1991. Information is available on nontraditional ways to
obtain financing. Chapters cover topics that include: receivables,
real estate, banks, government and even agricultural financing. The
authors offer more than 100 strategies for financing.

Dawson, George. *Borrowing for Your Business: Winning the Battle for the
Banker's "Yes."* Upstart Publishing, 1991.

■ Eight ■

Marketing Your Business

■

Marketing anticipates needs and directs the flow of goods and services from producers to consumers. As an entrepreneur, your mission is to target your product or service to the market that needs it. If your price is competitive (what the market will bear) and your product or service is valuable to your customer (because it has quality), you will achieve sales and repeat sales.

If you don't have a systematic method for getting your product to your customer and creating sufficient reason and urgency for that customer to buy, you have nothing. You might have the most perfectly structured business and the most needed product or service in your marketplace. You might even know who would buy your product. But, you still need a marketing strategy to tell your potential customer why he or she must buy *now*.

Marketing Strategies

It's important to create a mix of marketing strategies early in the development of your company. Your business plan broadly addressed the concept of marketing, it is now time to develop a detailed approach to marketing yourself and your business.

Your marketing plan will detail the strategies you need to use to promote your business in your specific market. It will also outline how you will apportion your advertising, direct sales (activities where you contact your market directly) and publicity campaigns (activities that utilize media exposure to reach your market). It will delineate the methods and tools you will use and in what general proportions you will address each of these areas in relation to time and monies spent. The plan will also address how you will maintain a balance of the four *Ps* we talked about earlier.

A very simple marketing plan might be based on the following outline:

- What marketing mix is offered to whom and for how long?
- What company resources/costs are required to do the job?
- What results are expected?
- What controls are needed to point out potential problems?

Marketing on a Shoestring

We know of very few smaller companies that have been able to start and grow their businesses without spending at least ten percent of their projected first-year revenues on marketing. Unless you are lucky and start with an existing client base, you need to spend time and money to build one. A little creativity can go a long way toward developing a successful small business marketing campaign. By mixing different strategies together, you can generate excitement.

Where should you begin? First, take the time to find out how companies similar to yours are marketing themselves. Successful marketing starts with committed dollars, but you need not overspend if you choose your strategies wisely. Move slowly. You will be inundated by salespeople urging you to advertise with them. Knowing what works in your market and what the costs are can save you hundreds, perhaps thousands of dollars. The first thing to do *before* you open your doors is to develop your yearly marketing plan. This plan lays out your monthly marketing mix. Keep to it as much as possible, making sure one strategy works into the next, and you will find that you will build customer awareness and readiness to buy much more quickly.

Public Relations—Your Best Strategy

Public relations begins with a clear definition of who you are, what niche you have chosen and a selection of tools that convey your message clearly. Everyone from the individual to the Fortune 100 corporation needs and uses public relations, and entrepreneurial businesses have a definite advantage. Because they are usually closer to their markets, entrepreneurs can react quickly to strengthen good relationships and correct misunderstandings before they get out of control.

The key to success with public relations lies in your ability to project a clear and purposeful message about who you are and what you have to offer. Remember . . . *Perception* is *Reality*.

Create an identity that cannot be mistaken by the public and develop an ongoing plan of action designed to reinforce your position in the market. Many businesses tend to continually create new corporate identities, shifting emphasis to suit temporary needs. That inconsistency can confuse customers, resulting in a dramatic drop in credibility and sales. Here are some pointers for keeping yourself—and your customers—focused:

- *Establish a consistent business identity.*   Press releases, business activities, choices of color, type styles, paper and other materials identified with your business must be in synch with your chosen identity. To be effective, they must convey one clear, unmistakable message.
- *Develop an aura of expertise and credibility.*   Any time you can obtain third-party endorsements, recommendations and referrals from satisfied customers your credibility is strengthened. When those endorsements appear in print, the public's perception of you is heightened.
- *Be involved in your industry.*   Activities such as writing for trade magazines and other media, public speaking,

workshops, seminars and radio/TV appearances position you as an authority. Demonstrate your expertise by serving on committees for organizations and associations where you are already a member.

- *Be professional and courteous when dealing with the media.* The media can help you maintain a high profile as long as you contribute something that will be newsworthy to their readers, viewers or listeners. Make it easy for the media to work with you by being dependable, agreeable and, most of all, resourceful.
- *Publicize yourself to customers.* In addition to using the media, consider publishing your own newsletter with news and views that would help clients. Send out mailings updating your qualifications at least four times a year. Write about new developments in your industry and how-to tips.

A successful public relations campaign is continuous and consistent. Although not easily measured, an effective campaign can give your business long-term credibility. Often you must work on public relations efforts for six months to a year before experiencing results. Too often, small business owners try new marketing and public relations strategies every other month and quit too soon—before reaping the benefits.

Tools of the Trade

The following resources can help you locate media assistance:

■ Resources

Name of Resource:	*Bacon's*
Where To Find It:	Bacon's Information, Inc.
	332 S. Michigan Ave.
	Chicago, IL 60604
	(312) 922-2400
	(800) 621-0561
Who Could Use It:	Any business
What It Contains:	*Bacon's Publicity Checker,* Vol. 1 lists 1,700 United States and Canadian dailies, and 8,100 United States weeklies with address, circulation, phone and fax numbers, ad rates for 1" column, plus editorial contact

information; including 31 editors and columnists by name at all dailies; 70,000 editors by name, news services/syndicates, syndicated columnists. Quarterly revisions.

Publicity Checker Magazines, Vol. 2 is a listing of more than 8,400 magazines with address, circulation, frequency, phone and fax numbers, ad rates for 1″ B & W and more. More than 40,000 editors are listed by name, arranged in more than 200 magazine classifications to target specific categories. Publicity codes show the type of releases accepted. Quarterly revisions.

Bacon's Radio/TV Directory—This complete listing of more than 10,000 U.S. radio and TV stations features call letters, phone and fax numbers, format programming, target audience, network affiliation and more; news, interview and discussion shows with contact names, show profiles; more than 65,000 key station contacts are provided by name. Lists include cable, syndicators, radio by format; maps of top 30 markets. Quarterly revisions.

Bacon's Media Alerts—These editorial calendars for major magazines and dailies contain editorial profiles and target audience information; editorial lead times for special issues; ad rates and closing dates; subject cross-index lists; additional placement opportunities; trade show index. Bimonthly updates.

Bacon's International Publicity Checker—The resource for contacting the Western European press contains more than 12,000 trade and business magazines and more than 1,000 newspapers; publicity codes that identify types of releases accepted, magazines divided into 64 categories; addressing samples for each country; translation requirements for news releases.

New—*Bacon's Business/Financial Directory*—This directory contains all business and financial editorial contacts for top newspapers, business magazines, radio and TV stations, news, talk and interview shows, target information for shows, expanded editorial staff listings at more than 250 business magazines; magazine editorial profiles; special indexes: subject "beat" index, all-media index, all-personnel index; more than 6,000 contacts at more than 1,000 outlets. Fully updated midyear edition.

Why Use It: Use if you want to develop a marketing program that is very targeted. Much less expensive and effective than taking out ad space, the directories cost approximately $200 apiece. Additional Bacon's services include a clipping bureau, mailing services and targeted media lists on either labels or IBM-compatible diskettes.

Name of Resource: Delphi General Videotex, Inc.
Where To Find It: 1030 Massachusetts Ave.
Cambridge, MA 02138
(617) 491-3393
(800) 544-4005
What It Contains: Will send broadcast business press releases electronically to specified telex, fax and electronic-mail lists
Why Use It: A service that will simplify your mailing process when you have press releases to disburse quickly and efficiently

Name of Resource: *Gale Directory of Publications and Broadcast Media*
Where To Find It: Gale Research Inc.
835 Penobscot Building
Detroit, MI 48226-4094
(800) 347-GALE
What It Contains: These two volumes contain detailed information on newspapers and magazines, and television, cable and radio stations in the United States, Puerto Rico and Canada.

Name of Resource: *Gebbie House Magazine Directory*—part of the *Working Press of Nations*

Where To Find It: National Research Bureau Headquarters
225 W. Wacker Dr.
Chicago, IL 60606
(312) 346-9097

What It Contains: Information on more than 100,000 media contacts including newsletters, house organs and internal company information

Name of Resource: *Newsclip's Illinois Media*—Updated annually and semiannually

Where To Find It: Your Public Library, or order directly from:
Newsclip
213 W. Institute Pl.
Chicago, IL 60610
(312) 751-7300
(312) 751-7316
FAX (312) 751-7306

What It Contains: A comprehensive directory of all print and electronic media in Illinois by classification and county, this resource contains addresses, phone numbers and contact persons.

Why Use It: It's a simple way to begin developing your own media list for local publicity.

When To Use It: When first setting up your mailing lists and for annual and semiannual updates

Name of Resource: PR News Service

Where To Find It: 35 E. Wacker Dr., Ste. 792
Chicago, IL 60601
(312) 782-8100

Who Could Use It: Any business

What It Contains: This service can send your press release to news bureaus, participating wire services, newspapers, radio and television stations, trade publications and databases.

Why Use It: The advantages of wire are speed and flexibility for people in media; format— your release goes right to a newsroom or feature desk. This is ideal for hard news

	that has to get out quickly. Bulk mail, such as you might send out for mass mailed news releases, can end up in the garbage.
When To Use It:	For news that is very timely, that needs to be released as soon as possible, i.e., a new product, an upcoming event, etc. The cost may be worth it.
Name of Resource:	*The Writer's Market*—(updated annually)
Where To Find It:	Your local library or bookstore
	Or order directly from:
	Writer's Digest Books
	1507 Dana Ave.
	Cincinnati, OH 45207
	(513) 531-2222
Who Could Use It:	Anyone interested in national exposure
What It Contains:	Suited for those who are interested in submitting business articles, *The Writer's Market* offers information on national publishers and the types of information they are most interested in receiving, including current contact person and preferred method of contact.
Why Use It:	It allows the most direct and accurate contact with decision-makers.

Press Releases

A successful campaign starts with a good press release—a one-page or two-page announcement that tells the media: *Who, What, Where, Why, When, How,* and *"So What."* It focuses on one major idea that the media's audience would find interesting, informative or newsworthy (or all of the above). A release is one of the most powerful small business tools available—and one that is most often misused. Here are some tips for creating successful press releases:

- Use the release to announce news in your business or industry, to establish your expertise and credibility.
- Address your releases to a specific editor. If you don't have a name, call and find out!

- Target the specific media most likely to be interested in your information. Don't get caught up thinking "more is better." You will have much better results if you target a few interested media outlets.
- Make sure your release offers newsworthy information (this is not the place to sell yourself). Follow industry trends: What types of businesses and issues are currently receiving extensive press coverage?
- Include a cover letter introducing your release and offering to be an information source for your areas of expertise.
- Keep your sentences short and easy to understand. You want your audience to read and quickly understand what you are saying.
- Standard format for releases is double-spaced with an inch to an inch and a half margin on all sides. This format is for the convenience of the editor. It makes the release easier to read and allows ample room for editors' notes and corrections.
- Write "News Release" in the upper left-hand corner and "For Immediate Release" or "For Release on (a specific date)" in the upper right-hand corner.
- Include a contact name and phone numbers during and after business hours. Writers have deadlines and frequently need to verify facts in a hurry.
- Signify the end of the release with "-30-" or "###."

Just as with any marketing strategy, repetition is key to your success. Be innovative. Look for great press ideas. If you are stumped for ideas, call the business editor of your local publications. (Don't forget to first ask when they would have a moment to talk.) Editors are always facing some deadline, but, for the most part, they are interested in receiving well-researched, interesting news. Ask them what they would like to receive—and then deliver it.

Below are a few ideas for generating news:

Stage a contest.	Promote someone.
Make a donation.	Do a good deed.
Conduct a survey.	Announce results of a survey.
Announce a new plan.	Organize a committee.
Make a progress report.	Take a stand on an issue.
Make a final report.	Hold a meeting/workshop.

Announce the visit of an	Turn a speech/leaflet into
out-of-town VIP.	a byline article.
Make a speech.	Provide "how-to" info.

Press Kits

While press releases are generally adequate for the entrepreneur's needs, there may be occasions to compile a press kit. Press kits are most effective when you offer a complex product or service or multiple lines. The kits provide your media contacts with background materials for current and future pieces about you and your company. Use the kits as a first contact with a media source and at press conferences. Kits usually include the following:

- Photos—use a variety. *Head* shots and *action* shots (black-and-white; sometimes four-color)
- Technical information (where appropriate)
- Background and historical facts about you and your company
- Biographical data sheets about you and your key personnel
- Human interest pieces—if directly related to the subject of your press kit
- Brochures—if applicable
- A copy of the press release
- Copies of published articles (the media like to see that you are newsworthy)
- Highlights of applicable speeches
- Direct quotes/testimonials/endorsements
- A list of anticipated questions/answers relating to the subject

Business Articles

While press releases describe your business and its news—business articles allow you to position yourself as an expert. Call the editors at your local newspapers or your trade magazines and ask if they could use articles about your area of expertise. You will be credited with a byline. Formats are typically the same as press releases although business articles can be longer than two pages, depending upon the editor's requirements. This marketing form can be very successful, especially for service-based companies. Even if you cannot write well, take advantage of the wealth of available writing talent through organizations for writers (e.g.,

Chicago Women in Publishing or Independent Writers of Chicago). A hired writer can either be a coauthor or a ghost writer (someone who writes the article but is not acknowledged). The latter arrangement is often used by successful business specialists.

One successful entrepreneur we know hired a ghost writer to help him write a series of articles about desktop publishing. He then offered the articles to a magazine free of charge, and promised additional information if they called him. The entrepreneur received many calls after the articles were published and gained clients as a result of his efforts. This is a good example of smart marketing. Although the entrepreneur had to spend some time and money up-front, it was nominal.

Flyers

Flyers are inexpensive promotional pieces generally used as hand-out or throw-away items. They may be given personally to prospective customers, placed on car windshields, inserted in mass distributed pieces such as newspapers, bulletins and newsletters, attached to doorways, etc. They usually contain a brief message: What you offer and where you can be found. In general, flyers feature a bold eye-catching headline, graphics or pictures, a message and directions on how to reach you. They frequently include a discount coupon to encourage follow-up.

Generally the simplest, least expensive method for flooding a specific area with information, flyers are best used when announcing sales or special offers, or promoting inexpensive products/services.

Brochures

Brochures are usually 8 1/2" x 11" or 11" x 17", three-fold or four-fold pieces. Two-colored, three-colored or four-colored, brochures are much more expensive than flyers. Typically handed personally to prospects or mailed to a targeted group, brochures can also be left at a distribution point, such as a store counter, to draw attention and to be picked up.

A brochure, while using fewer words than you would need in a personal contact, allows you to tell your story in great detail. It may focus on your business, any of your products or services, or on individuals within the organization. It may also be strictly an information piece.

Particularly valuable to service companies, brochures serve as a tangible piece of the business that creates credibility and brings about a sale. Typically you will want to include enough in your brochure to tell the whole story, but not enough to confuse the reader. Keep it simple and direct, and focus on customer benefits. Promotional pieces often include some or all of the following information:

- Business name/your name
- Business address
- Telephone and fax numbers
- Contact person (if other than yourself)
- Photos/drawings of product or representation of service
- Description of your product or service
- Price list (indicate if wholesale or retail)
- Terms of payment
- Return policy
- Shipping terms
- Minimum order policy (dollar or unit amount)
- Warranties and/or guarantees

A brochure allows you to tell your story completely and create further interest on the part of the reader. It should clearly demonstrate your expertise, attention to detail and understanding of your customers' needs. Be sure to design your brochure in such a way that it does not need to be changed frequently.

Newsletters

This marketing tool generally serves two purposes: first, to target a specific readership or market and second, to establish you as the expert that your readers will turn to when they require your services or product.

Newsletters are good for delivering hard news relevant to your business, products or services. Talk to your customers to find out the kind of information they might be looking for. Read through several of your industry's trade journals to stay current on industry trends and to get ideas for your own articles.

Create your newsletter with a blend of hard news relative to your industry/product and soft news—information on your company's goals and objectives and information on programs and projects. Establish what you hope to accomplish through this publication and who your readers will be. Then write for them. If you really understand your customers, it's relatively easy to find materials of interest to them. When you fill your newsletter with news your readers want to read, you will be building your credibility and establishing yourself as an expert.

To create winning newsletters, be sure that you have a clear-cut written statement of objectives and editorial policy *before* beginning. These publications should be used any time you wish to establish a regular method of communication with a targeted readership. *But remember:* This is not a one-time project. The effectiveness of this method of promotion relies heavily on consistency. Consider mailing at least quarterly. And, most importantly, don't attempt this unless you have studied the process and techniques extensively or have expert assistance. A poorly designed newsletter can do more harm than good.

If you're serious about taking the do-it-yourself approach, don't let anyone discourage you, *but* be prepared for major investments of money and time. Begin by getting proper training. There are several excellent publishing and/or desktop publishing courses available throughout the Chicagoland area.

■ Resources

Name of Resource:	Chicago Book Clinic
Where To Find It:	111 E. Wacker Dr., Ste. 200
	Chicago, IL 60601
	(312) 946-1700
Who Could Use It:	Anyone interested in the production of newsletters and other promotional pieces and desktop publishing
What It Contains:	This professional publishing education program features courses and seminars taught on the Chicago campus of Northwestern University. Topics cover everything from pre-press and job specifications to color separation and film assembly.
Why Use It:	A valuable source essential for professional production of public relations pieces
When To Use It:	When you plan to be directly involved in the production of your promotional pieces

Name of Resource:	Dynamic Graphics Educational Foundation
Where To Find It:	6000 N. Forest Park Dr.
	Peoria, IL 61614
	(800) 255-8800
	(309) 688-5873 (FAX)
Who Could Use It:	Anyone who plans to invest substantial time and energy in desktop publishing for their business
What It Contains:	Specialized courses are offered in all facets of graphics and print media. Also an excellent source for clip art, Dynamic Graphics publishes: *Step-by-Step Graphics*, a bimonthly magazine, and *Step-by-Step Electronic Design*, a monthly newsletter offering practical how-to information for the communications expert.
Why Use It:	If you plan to produce your own newsletter, you can't afford to let it reflect anything but your best image.

■

Publication

The Professional Look: The Complete Guide to Desktop Publishing, Stephen E. Mancuso and Scott W. Tilden. Venture Perspectives Press, (805) 967-5184. An excellent resource on publishing and desktop publishing—from purchasing equipment and software to preparing camera-ready pieces and working with printers.

Speaking Engagements

Opportunities for speaking engagements include workshops, seminars, association meetings and radio and TV talk shows. Speaking before area groups can increase a business's revenues 20 percent or more. Search for speaking opportunities everywhere. Welcome invitations. Be creative.

Keep a file on area clubs that schedule speakers and contact them early. September and October are excellent times to contact incoming officers to arrange a program during their tenure. Take the time to write a one-page biography. Get a professional photographer to take your picture, and then have a printer typeset and design a professional presentation piece. Include two or three titles of speeches you could give. In the meantime, create outlines for these speeches and include this sheet as part of your press kit.

Speaking engagements are particularly effective because they allow you to maintain high visibility, recognition and credibility within the group. Such opportunities allow you to demonstrate your expertise and expand your exposure in well-defined market segments. The invitation to be a guest speaker says to your audience that you have the organization's endorsement.

Conventions

Trade shows are one of the best marketing strategies for entrepreneurs because they offer one-stop opportunities to sell. For the price of a booth design (if necessary) and the booth rental fee, you are exposed to a targeted audience—prospects who are attending the show for the express purpose of buying the types of products or services that you sell.

All shows are not created equal. It is up to you to do some research to determine which trade shows would be best for you. For information on trade shows held in Chicago, contact the Chicago Convention and Tourism Bureau, Inc., McCormick Place-on-the-Lake, (312) 567-3855. Additional information on trade shows at specific trade show centers follows:

■ Resources _____

Name of Resource:	Chicago/South Expo Center
Where To Find It:	Harvey, IL 60426
	(708) 331-4265
What It Contains:	Located 25 minutes south of the Chicago Loop, this 30,000-square-foot facility features meeting rooms that can accommodate 250-300 people.
Name of Resource:	Expocenter/Chicago
Where To Find It:	350 N. Orleans St.
	Chicago, IL 60654
	(312) 527-7640
What It Contains:	Part of the Merchandise Mart Properties, owned by the Kennedy family, this 140,000-square-foot facility is the largest privately

owned exhibit center in the United States. Expocenter/Merchandise Market is the home of the world's largest Contract Furnishing Show—NeoCon, as well as the largest Casual Furniture Market, Apparel Shows and Gift Markets.

Name of Resource: McCormick Place
Where To Find It: 2301 S. Lake Shore Dr.
Chicago, IL 60616
(312) 791-7000
What It Contains: The largest exposition center in the United States, McCormick Place has over 1.6 million square feet of available exhibit space.

Name of Resource: Rosemont/O'Hare Exposition Center
Where To Find It: 5555 N. River Rd.
Rosemont, IL 60018
(708) 692-2220
What It Contains: This 450,000-square-foot convention/exhibition facility is located just five minutes from O'Hare airport.

Name of Resource: *Trade Shows & Exhibits Guide*
Where To Find It: Sales and Marketing
633 Third Ave., 34th Fl.
New York, NY 10002
(800) 253-6708
What It Contains: This listing, updated annually, of more than 11,000 exhibitions worldwide, is indexed by industry, profession, date and geographical region. A midyear supplement is provided.

Name of Resource: *Trade Shows & Professional Exhibits Directory List*
Where To Find It: Gale Research Inc.
835 Penobscot Building
Detroit, MI 48226-4094
(313) 961-3707
What It Contains: This directory contains a comprehensive list of trade shows, exhibits, conventions, meetings, as well as trade and industrial shows throughout the United States.

Why Use It: To identify shows where you might exhibit

-- ■

The key to your success is to keep your name in front of your customer at all times—not to impress them, but to keep reminding them that you are there.

Everyday Business Practices

Whenever you write a letter or pick up the phone you are presenting yourself to the public. Don't underestimate the power of these communications. Many people lack confidence in their ability to write letters—a regular and important occurrence in every business. Take the time to make sure you have a clean, concise letter that asks for something—a call to action. Use the books listed below as guides to writing great business letters. You don't need to copy each word of the samples. Just let the ideas help you create your own effective written communication style.

Publications

Booher, Dianna. *Letter Perfect, A Handbook of Model Letters for the Busy Executive.* Lexington Books, 1988.

Nicholas, Ted. *The Executive's Business Letter Book.* Dearborn Financial Publishing, 1992.

Poe, Roy. *McGraw-Hill Handbook of Business Letters.* McGraw-Hill, 1991.

Van Dyn, J. A., editor, *Director's and Officer's Complete Letter Book,* second edition. Prentice Hall, 1983.

Advertising

Advertising is a method of reaching potential customers that requires payment for placement of your message in print, radio or television media. This marketing strategy focuses on the product or service you offer and openly solicits action on the part of the reader/listener/viewer. Since advertising represents a major portion of your marketing budget, it is critical that you keep your message brief and to the point.

The less visible you are, the more you need advertising to keep your name in front of the public. Establish a routine—smaller advertisements placed frequently are more effective than one big splash. Be sure your ad contains a clear message: who you are, what you're offering, how you can be reached, as well as a request for action.

One form of advertising frequently taken for granted, is the *Yellow Pages*. This can be an extremely effective tool if your ads are carefully thought out and well-constructed. *Yellow Pages* ads can be terribly expensive, but they have the advantage of targeting *warm* customers. Callers responding to *Yellow Pages* ads typically are in the market for your product or service. Keep in mind that your *Yellow Pages* ad will be surrounded by your competition's ads. Make sure that your ad conveys a sense of urgency and uniqueness. If your market research indicates that *Yellow Pages* advertising is good for your type of business, consider a relatively large ad (at least 1" x 1") placed, if possible, in the upper right-hand corner of the book.

Direct Mail

Direct mail can be used whenever you want to reach a particular individual or class of individuals. It is an extremely effective tool for entrepreneurs. Direct mail includes:

Fact sheets	Letters
Promotional giveaways	Contests
Discount coupons	Brochures

Mailing lists are the backbone of your promotional efforts. Buy them, rent them, maintain your own. They're priceless and virtually irreplaceable. But don't expect more than a two percent response. That's the national average. Target your market by age, sex, ethnic background, education, occupation, family status and income. Analyze the lifestyle, personal behavior and values, community involvement, ambition, skepticism, self-concept, buying style and itch cycle (that cycle that typifies their buying habits) of your chosen market. And be aware of current trends and fads.

Use direct mail to introduce yourself and your product, solicit mail-order/phone orders, announce new products/services, notify customers of price changes, welcome new customers, thank current customers and highlight special events. Target your audience with broker lists. Direct mail specialists say that the list is the most important part of a direct mail campaign. Either compile your own list by using the directories mentioned in Chapter 4, and the media resources listed on pages 114-118 of this chapter, or contact a list broker—a professional who compiles, updates and sells lists. A good list broker will be able to compile almost any kind of list imaginable.

A list targeted to a specific segment of the market decreases costs and increases the possibility of reaching potential customers who should be most receptive to your product. If you are planning to do any direct mail marketing, it is worthwhile to at least talk to a list broker. You can obtain names of brokers from your local telephone directory or by calling the Chicago Direct Marketing Association at (312) 922-6222.

Ask the post office about their business mailer services (CD-ROM and Operation Mail). You must be familiar with mailing regulations—particularly when using bulk rate mailing. First class mailings typically get better response; however, bulk rate mailings can be effective for continuous mailings. Your post office is a valuable resource when you decide to use direct mail as a means of marketing. Take the time to confer with your postmaster concerning your plans; he or she may be able to suggest cost-efficient alternatives you hadn't considered. The post office offers publications and brochures explaining guidelines and other time and money-saving techniques.

■ Resources

Name of Resource:	*Direct Mail List, Rates and Data*
Where To Find It:	Your library or Standard Rate and Data Service 3004 Glenview Rd. Wilmette, IL 60091 (708) 256-6067
What It Contains:	A compilation of thousands of companies that sell mailing lists featuring subject and market classification references, titles and owner company identifications in alphabetical order
Why Use It:	For targeting new clients, telemarketing, direct mail campaigns, etc.
When To Use It:	Any time you require a specific prospect

list in a specific categorical breakdown

Name of Resource:	*The National Directory of Mailing Lists*
Where To Find It:	Your library or
	Oxbridge Communications
	150 Fifth Ave.
	New York, NY 10011
	(212) 741-0231
What It Contains:	This annually updated reference guide cites more than 33,000 mailing lists in the United States and Canada divided by categories. It includes concise descriptions and names of key list personnel (circulation director, list manager, account manager).
Why Use It:	For targeting new clients, telemarketing, direct mail campaigns, etc.
When To Use It:	Any time you require a specific prospect list in a specific categorical breakdown

————————————————— ■

Making the Sale

The goal of all your marketing efforts is to make the sale. *Sales ability* is critical to your continued growth—the most important skill you could have. Larger companies usually employ many people to promote their products. In a smaller business, you may do this yourself, hire a full-time salesperson or work with an independent contractor—offering paid commissions based on sales volume.

If you are not comfortable with sales, or find that you need to sharpen your skills, we highly recommend taking sales training courses. Ask around for referrals to trainers specializing in small business sales. Although selling techniques are rather universal, it is important to learn from others who have been involved in selling the services of a company similar to your own.

Even if you had a great track record with a previous employer, you will find entrepreneurial sales to be very different. As an entrepreneur you represent yourself—not an established business. Thus, it is important that your sales tools (brochures, slides, etc.) support *who you are* and *what you can do* for the customer.

You don't necessarily need lots of customers—just the right

ones. If you have taken the time to identify your market, its need *and* its willingness to pay to satisfy that need, you should be able to pull in a minimal number of clients with a maximum payoff.

Whether you are in high-volume (product-oriented) or low-volume (service-oriented) sales, it's a numbers game. Use the 80-20 rule—80 percent of your business will come from 20 percent of your clients. Sell to those larger, potential clients in your targeted niche markets. If you have taken the time to locate that market and you are prepared, your sales success ratio could be one client for every five to ten sales calls (or even better).

Customer Service—The Key to Repeat Sales

A lot has been written about customer service. The bottom line is that keeping customers is crucial to your long-term success. Following are some basic tips for keeping your customers happy and loyal:

- *Have a plan.*   It will help you follow through and achieve tangible and quantifiable results.
- *Use a questionnaire to follow up after a sale.*   The questionnaire should address the level of satisfaction the customer had after using your product or service. The benefits of the questionnaire are two-fold. First, questionnaires that offer favorable comments can serve as references leading to better sales results. Second, those that offer criticism can provide feedback to improve sales techniques that can also lead to more sales.
- *Take the time to call your customers regularly.*   This technique can be extremely effective—yet many small business owners make the mistake of not considering current customers for new sales opportunities. Experts have shown that it is much easier to secure new sales through existing customers than new ones. One entrepreneur we know contacts her current customers at least once a week and her past customers at least once a month.

Customers who are truly satisfied with what you have done for them will use you again and again, and often refer you to others. If you've pleased a customer, ask them to give you referrals and testimonials that you can use in your promotions.

Referrals are critical to your growth and are one of the very best marketing tools. Once you have provided the first customer with service beyond expectations (under-promise and over-deliver), it will be easier to get new customers.

Where To Get Help

Depending on how deeply involved you choose to be in the production and processing of your promotional materials, you may want to seek the guidance and expertise of professionals. Promotion—advertising and public relations—is a never-ending process. This is the one area of your business where you cannot afford to cut corners. Particularly when the economy is tight—as it has been in the last year or so—you need to put energy and dollars into conveying your messages to the public. Many fine organizations, training programs, seminars and publications are available to help you in this endeavor. The following resources will stand you in good stead and get you started on the right foot:

■ Resources _____

Name of Resource:	American Marketing Association
Where To Find It:	250 S. Wacker Dr., Ste. 200
	Chicago, IL 60606
	(312) 648-0536
Who Could Use It:	Anyone actively involved in marketing a business
What It Contains:	With more than 400 local chapters, this organization can be a great resource for full-time and part-time marketing professionals. The association holds regular meetings that feature targeted seminars and well-known speakers. Members also receive a directory of nearly 30,000 professional and executive members in the fields of advertising, sales, sales management, retail sales and education. Additional services include telephone support, on-line data searches and an information center.
Name of Resource:	Direct Marketing Association (DMA)
Where To Find It:	11 W. 42nd St.

	New York, NY 10036-8096 (212) 768-7277 or (312) 922-6222 in Chicago
Who Could Use It:	Any business that focuses promotion and sales in areas of direct mail
What It Contains:	The DMA holds regular seminars on creating successful direct mail marketing plans. It also offers services that help small businesses reduce the volume of unwanted advertising mail and a mail-order action line that helps those with mail-order problems. A monthly newsletter is available to members.

Publications

Levinson, Jay Conrad. *Guerrilla Marketing Attack: New Strategies, Tactics and Weapons for Winning Big Profits for Your Small Business.* Houghton Mifflin, 1989.

O'Dwyer's Director of Public Relations Firms. J.R. O'Dwyer Co. (updated yearly).

Phillips, Michael and Salli Rasberry. *Marketing Without Advertising.* Nolo Press, 1986.

Public Relations Journal—Directory Issue. Public Relations Society of America, (updated yearly).

Rapp, Stan and Tom Collins. *Max/Marketing: The New Direction in Advertising, Promotion and Marketing Strategy.* McGraw-Hill, 1987.

Ries, Al and Jack Trout. *Marketing Warfare.* McGraw-Hill, 1986.

Ries, Al. *Positioning: The Battle for Your Mind.* McGraw-Hill, 1989.

The following publications are available from the Illinois Business Hotline at (800) 252-2923. Call for a current SBA Directory of Business Development marketing publications, which will include the following:

- *Advertising* Learn how you can effectively market products and services.
- *Creative Selling the Competitive Edge* An explanation of how to use creative selling techniques to increase profits.
- *Marketing for Small Business* This overview of marketing

concepts contains an extensive bibliography of sources covering the subject of marketing.

- *Marketing Checklist for Small Retailers*   This checklist is for the owner/manager of a small retail business. It outlines questions covering customer analysis, buying, pricing and promotion, and other factors in the retail marketing process.
- *Selling by Mail Order*   A compendium of basic information on how to run a successful mail order business, this publication includes information on product selection, pricing, testing and writing effective advertisements.

■ Nine ■

Government and Educational Resources

■

Both federal and state governments offer entrepreneurs a variety of assistance—from counseling, to seminars, to funding resources. During the last year alone, Illinois has become much more involved in an effort to address the needs of its growing number of small businesses. In this chapter we provide a list of federal, state and educational resources.

Federal Assistance

As mentioned in earlier chapters, the Small Business Administration (SBA) offers several useful services to the entrepreneur, including educational publications and one-on-one counseling available through the Service Core of Retired Executives (SCORE). We recommend that you first seek general assistance from state-run agencies such as the small business development centers and then request specific business information from SCORE counselors. We have found that most of the SCORE counselors are experts in particular fields; it will be more beneficial if you work with them after you have an idea of the support you will need.

Conveniently located in the Loop, the SBA offers very reasonable workshops that can be of great help to entrepreneurs. Realize that working with the government is similar to working with any business assistance specialist—it involves a one-on-one relationship. If you find that one person cannot help you as much as you had hoped, find someone else. The SBA has many experienced people ready and willing to help you. Contact the numbers below for further information:

■ Resources _____

Name of Resource:	Business Assistance Service
Where To Find It:	Office of Business Liaison
	U.S. Department of Commerce
	14th & Constitution, Rm. 5898-C
	Washington, DC 20230
	(202) 377-3176
	Region V Offices
	CNA Bldg., Rm. 1402
	55 E. Jackson Blvd.
	Chicago, IL 60604
	(312) 353-8143
What It Contains:	Set up to help guide small businesses through the federal maze, this resource can help you locate the federal agency best able to serve your particular needs. *The Business Services Directory*, which lists the agency's many services, can be ordered through this number.
When To Use It:	Whenever you need help locating federal agencies that might service your needs
Name of Resource:	Federal Information Center
Where To Find It:	PO Box 600
	Cumberland, MD 21501-0600
	(800) 366-2998
What It Contains:	This is the main referral/information center for the federal government. It provides assistance for individuals looking for the

phone numbers for particular government agencies, and also houses a special assistance staff and research department that answers government-related questions.

Name of Resource:	Service Core of Retired Executives (SCORE)
Where To Find It:	Call the Illinois Business Hotline at (800) 252-2923 for locations.
Who Could Use It:	Any manufacturing-oriented business
What It Contains:	Upon request, counseling from experts in your particular field
Why Use It:	This is a great resource, particularly if you can find a retired executive who has expertise in your type of business. Valuable information is available at no charge.

Name of Resource:	Small Business Administration (SBA)—Answer Desk
Where To Find It:	(800) 827-5722
What It Contains:	This prerecorded information base concerns all facets of business—from start-up and financing programs to international trade. Several messages are available. Publications offered by the SBA may be ordered by calling this number.
Why Use It:	To obtain information on federal programs and available financing and to request information on specific topics specifically directed to small business needs

Name of Resource:	Small Business Administration (SBA)—Federal Government
Where To Find It:	Federal Building 219 S. Dearborn, Rm. 437 Chicago, IL 60604 (312) 353-4528 (800) 368-5899
What It Contains:	This office provides counseling through SCORE, assistance programs such as the Management and Technical Assistance Program (listed below) and numerous publications on all facets of business.

Why Use It: This is an excellent resource for small businesses to obtain information, counseling and guidance concerning all facets of doing business.

Income Tax Assistance

Name of Resource: Internal Revenue Service Taxpayer Hotline Taxpayer Information and Education Branch

Where To Find It: Taxpayer Service Division
1111 Constitution Ave., N.W.
Washington, DC 20224
(800) 829-1040

What It Contains: The hotline is the place to go for answers to such questions as: How much can you deduct for business meals? How much can you deduct for a home-based business? How much can you deduct for travel expenses? You can also order a Federal Employer Identification Number (FEIN), an updated Small Business Tax Guide or Start-Up Kit through the hotline.

Why Use It: For information regarding tax returns and for tax planning

Name of Resource: U.S. Department of Labor

Where To Find It: 230 S. Dearborn
Chicago, IL 60604
(312) 353-0313

What It Contains: Information concerning labor/employment issues—particularly those that fall within the jurisdiction of the federal government

Government Publications

Name of Resource: Federal Government Bookstore

Where To Find It: 401 S. State St., Ste. 124
Chicago, IL 60605
(312) 353-5133

What It Contains: Open from 8:30 A.M. to 4:00 P.M. Monday through Friday, this bookstore sells numerous government publications.

Why Use It: An excellent resource for obtaining government publications

Name of Resource: *SBA Directory of Business Development Publications*
Where To Find It: (800) 827-5722
What It Contains: Each book costs between $ .50 and $2. Don't let the low cost fool you. You are actually paying what the SBA terms a "donation" because the books are very complete and helpful. The following list of available publications is reprinted from an order form called "SBA Business Development."

Reducing Shoplifting Losses   Learn the latest techniques on how to spot, deter, apprehend and prosecute shoplifters.

Crime—Inside and Out   Positive steps can be taken to curb crime. They include safeguards against employee dishonesty and ways to control shoplifting. In addition, this publication includes measures on how to outwit bad check passing and ways to prevent burglary and robbery.

A Small Business Guide to Computer Security   This publication helps you understand the nature of computer security risks and offers advice on how to control them.
Why Use It: An excellent resource for expert advice and information

Special Federal Programs for Disadvantaged Individuals

Name of Resource: Management and Technical Assistance Program
Where To Find It: Small Business Administration
(312) 353-9098
Office of Minority Small Business & Capital Ownership Development
Div. of Management & Technical Assistance
Ask for:
Request for Counseling, SBA Form 641
The Facts About Management and Technical Assistance 7(j) Program
List of Current Service Providers

Who Could Use It: SBA 8(a)-certified firms, socially and economically disadvantaged persons/businesses operating in areas of low income or high unemployment and firms owned by low-income individuals are eligible.

Professional management assistance firms that have been in business at least one year prior to the closing date for submitting proposals and have a staff capacity to perform at least 55 percent of the work may submit proposals to provide management and technical assistance to socially and economically disadvantaged individuals and businesses. Awardees are selected by SBA specialists based on such factors as previous experience and performance effectiveness, staff capability and quality.

What It Contains: This program provides linkage between qualified established businesses and disadvantaged individuals and businesses in the areas of bookkeeping and accounting services, production, engineering/technical advice, feasibility studies, market analyses and advertising expertise, limited legal services and specialized management training. Many of the services are free.

Why Use It: If economically and socially disadvantaged, this is a resource for technical assistance.

Established businesses who are experienced and looking for opportunities to expand will find this a source of new business.

Financial Assistance

Name of Resource: Government Programs and Loans

Where To Find It: Small Business Administration
Office of Financial Institutions
Washington, DC 20416
(202) 634-1500, or call local or regional SBA offices for an institution near you.

What It Contains: The SBA will provide a list of the 650 lenders in its Certified Lender or Preferred Lender Program.

Why Use It: To identify local participating lenders

-- ■

State Assistance

The Illinois Department of Commerce and Community Affairs (DCCA) is really a network of centers located around the state to provide business management, counseling and training, and assistance in entering international markets. Information on competing for state and federal contracts, developing technology-related products and providing a supportive environment for new businesses is also available. The network consists of Small Business Development Centers, Procurement Assistance Centers, Small Business Incubators and International Trade Centers. DCCA has a toll-free number to help you with a variety of business concerns. Call the Illinois Business Hotline (800) 252-2923 to obtain information about the following areas:

- Small business start-up kits
- Preparing business and marketing plans
- Securing capital
- Improving business skills
- Accessing international trade opportunities
- Contract procurement
- Economics and programs within Illinois
- Technology commercialization centers
- Small business incubators

Illinois assistance centers are strategically located throughout the state. Independently contracted with DCCA, these information storehouses provide guidance and assistance to emerging business. Three distinct programs are available through this network, although not all programs are available at every location:

SBDCs (Small Business Development Centers)   These centers offer assistance in identifying a business's needs, help with developing a business plan, offer counseling concerning financing and provide referrals to resources.

PACs (Procurement Assistance Centers)   These centers, which carry copies of state bid lists and forms, as well as the *Illinois Courier,* can help you to develop a working relationship with the government.

ITCs (International Trade Centers)   An excellent resource for those interested in international trade.

Call DCCA's Small Business Hotline to obtain the name of the center that serves your community. Centers and the programs they provide include:

Back of the Yards Neighbor-
hood Council (SBDC)
1751 W. 47th St.
Chicago, IL 60609
(312) 523-4419

CANDO (SBDC)
343 S. Dearborn St., Ste. 910
Chicago, IL 60604-3808
(312) 939-7235

City Colleges of Chicago (PAC)
226 W. Jackson Blvd., 4th Fl.
Chicago, IL 60606
(312) 368-8844

College of DuPage (SBDC)
(PAC) (ITC)
22nd and Lambert Rd.
Glen Ellyn, IL 60137
(708) 858-2800 (SBDC, ext. 2771)
(PAC, ext. 2184) (ITC, ext. 3052)

College of Lake County (SBDC)
(PAC)
19351 W. Washington St.
Grayslake, IL 60030
(708) 223-3633 (SBDC)
(708) 223-3612 (PAC)

DCCA State of Illinois Center
100 W. Randolph, Ste. 3-400
Chicago, IL 60601
(312) 814-2829

Eighteenth Street Development
Corporation (SBDC)
1839 S. Carpenter
Chicago, IL 60608
(312) 733-2287

Elgin Community College
(SBDC)
1700 Spartan Dr.
Elgin, IL 60123
(708) 697-1000 (SBDC, ext. 7923)

Evanston Business & Technology Center (SBDC) (SET)
1840 Oak Ave.
Evanston, IL 60201
(708) 864-0800
FAX (708) 866-1808 (SBDC)

Governors State University
(SBDC)
University Park, IL 60466
(708) 534-4929

Greater North Pulaski Economic Development Commis-
sion (SBDC) Small Business Development Center
4054 W. North Ave.
Chicago, IL 60639
(312) 384-2262

Latin American Chamber of
Commerce (SBDC) (PAC)
2539 N. Kedzie, Ste. 11

Chicago, IL 60647
(312) 252-5211
Loop SBDC (SBDC) (PAC)

McHenry County College
(SBDC)
8900 U.S. Hwy. 14
Crystal Lake, IL 60012
(815) 455-8783

Moraine Valley College (SBDC)
(SET) (PAC)
10900 S. 88th Ave.
Palos Hills, IL 60465
(708) 974-5468 (SBDC & SET)
(708) 974-5452 (PAC)

Olive-Harvey College (SBDC)
10001 S. Woodlawn Ave.
Chicago, IL 60628
(312) 660-4839

South Suburban College (PAC)
15800 S. State St.
South Holland, IL 60473
(708) 596-2000

Triton/Morton Colleges
(SBDC)
2000 Fifth Ave.
River Grove, IL 60171
(708) 456-0300

Waubonsee Community College (SBDC)—Aurora Campus
5 E. Galena Blvd.
Aurora, IL 60506
(708) 892-3334 (SBDC, ext. 141)
(PAC, ext. 139)

William Rainey Harper College
(SBDC)
1200 W. Algonquin Rd.
Palatine, IL 60067
(708) 397-3000

Women's Business Development Center (SBDC)
8 S. Michigan Ave., Ste. 400
Chicago, IL 60603
(312) 853-3477

DCCA's Small Business Assistance Bureau's Business Development Division administers programs throughout Illinois to assist existing small businesses and start-ups in the following areas:

The Procurement Assistance Program consists of a network of 17 centers statewide that help companies through all phases of bidding on and securing a government contract.

The Technology Commercialization Center provides research assistance, new product feasibility studies and product testing to new entrepreneurs.

The Small Business Innovation Research Program provides funds for developing a commercial product from technological research that a company has completed.

The Illinois Product and Services Exchange Program refers large firms to small, local suppliers of goods and services rather than out-of-state suppliers.

The Small Business Incubator Program provides management assistance, shared office resources and affordable space to existing and start-up businesses.

The Small Business Trade Assistance Program provides information and assistance to businesses interested in exporting their products. This office administers the state's small business development centers.

For more information on the Small Business Assistance Bureau, call the Illinois Business Hotline (800) 252-2923, or (217) 524-5856.

Note: For further information, consider ordering *Starting a Small Business in Illinois,* a publication of the Illinois Business Development Center Network available through the Illinois Business Hotline. This is a comprehensive compilation of resources, as well as requirements, regulations and other aspects of operating a business in the state. It includes listings of state agencies that you can call for additional information and updates.

■ Resources _____

Special State Programs for Disadvantaged Individuals

Name of Resource:	Self-Employment Education and Development (SEED)
Where To Find It:	Private Industry Council of Northern Cook County 2604 E. Dempster, Ste. 502 Des Plaines, IL 60016 (708) 699-9040
Who Could Use It:	SEED helps unemployed Chicago workers affected by plant closings and layoffs. Participants have solid work histories—they range from production workers to upper management personnel who have found themselves unexpectedly unemployed. Many have thought of becoming self-employed and use this opportunity to try entrepreneurial life.
What It Contains:	This program includes skills analysis,

	business skills training and assistance in assessing and planning a business. Participants are also given individual guidance sessions.
Why Use It:	It is an excellent, free program.
When To Use It:	Upon notification of a layoff

Name of Resource:	Self Employment Training (SET)
Where To Find It:	Private Industry Council (PIC) of Northern Cook County 2604 E. Dempster, Ste. 502 Des Plaines, IL 60016 (708) 699-9040
Who Could Use It:	If you are unemployed or consider yourself underemployed
Why Use It:	This program is provided at no cost to qualified applicants. Funding is made available to PIC from DCCA.
What It Contains:	SET provides a comprehensive, ten-week program for start-ups that includes marketing, management, business planning and finance. The course also provides approximately five hours of one-on-one counseling with seasoned entrepreneurs.
When To Use It:	Prior to start-up or within the first six months of start-up

■

Note: Other PICs that might have similar programs are:

DuPage County PIC serving DuPage County (708) 682-7884
KDK Training, Employment and Business Services serving the tri-county area of Kane, DeKalb and Kendall (708) 232-5920
Will County PIC serving the northern Will County area (815) 886-5055

State Assistance for Women Business Owners

Illinois is home to one of the few Women's Business Advocates—Mollie Cole—whose office is in the Loop:

Department of Commerce & Community Affairs (DCCA)
100 W. Randolph St., Ste. 3-400
Chicago, IL 60601
(312) 814-7179

Mollie Cole supports the needs of women business owners in Illinois through the development of women's business councils. Five councils have been formed in downstate Illinois, and The Chicago Suburban Women's Business Council has very recently been formed in the Chicago suburbs. For information about this and other councils, contact Ms. Cole.

If you are a business owner looking for "the organization or seminar" that will help you grow your business, the Women's Business Advocate publishes a bi-monthly *Women's Business Calendar of Events*. For a complimentary copy, write Women's Business Advocate, Illinois Department of Commerce and Community Affairs, 100 W. Randolph, S3-400, Chicago, IL 60601.

Small Business Development Centers

The following resources sponsored by educational institutions, offer various forms of business assistance, sometimes with government funding.

■ **Resources** _____

Technological and Manufacturing Resource Assistance Centers

Name of Resource:	Chicago Technology Park, Corporate Incubator
Where To Find It:	2201 W. Campbell Park Dr.
	Chicago, IL 60612
	(312) 829-7252 or (800) 843-1441
	FAX (312) 829-4069
Who Could Use It:	Science-based companies
What It Contains:	This incubator seeks to coordinate industry, university and government partnerships to stimulate the formation of science-based companies and economic development in the Chicago area. It provides access to university and hospital resources, offers assistance in the creation of new venture companies and provides space in an incubator building.
Why Use It:	For financial and support resources

Name of Resource: College of DuPage
Where To Find It: Technology Commercialization Center
Business and Professional Institute
22nd & Lambert Rd.
Glen Ellyn, IL 60137-6599
(708) 858-6870
(708) 858-2800 ext. 2948
Dept. of Cont. Ed. (708) 858-7148
What It Contains: This center links high-technology businesses to the university and other resources
to assist in the production and commercialization of new ideas and products and
to enhance the transfer of technologies
from university laboratories into the marketplace. It sponsors training seminars,
workshops and conferences, and offers
monthly economic development breakfasts for the business community.

Name of Resource: Evanston Research Park
Where To Find It: Northwestern University
1710 Orrington Ave.
Evanston, IL 60201
(708) 475-7170
What It Contains: The research park encourages the exchange
of activities between the university and
park tenants and transfers technological
advances to basic industry. Current tenants include the Basic Industry Research
Laboratory of Northwestern University,
which focuses on manufacturing and applied materials research, the Institute for
Learning Sciences and Artificial Intelligence
Center, and the Computer-Integrated Manufacturing Demonstration Center. The park
provides a small business incubator system
to support newly developing, high-technology companies, offers technical assistance and administers a seed capital fund.
Why Use It: Provides general business assistance
When To Use It: Prior to start-up and after

Name of Resource: Technology Commercialization Center
Where To Find It: Northern Illinois University
                           DeKalb, IL 60115-2874
                           (815) 753-1238
                           FAX (815) 753-2305
What It Contains: This center administers the interdiscipli-
                           nary research service centers of the univer-
                           sity, including machine shops, a glass shop,
                           liquid helium and liquid nitrogen facilities
                           and a biotechnology research and service
                           facility. Support is provided for interdisci-
                           plinary research centers.

Name of Resource: Technology Commercialization Center
Where To Find It: Stuart School of Business Bldg., Rm. 229 B
                           Chicago, IL 60616
                           (312) 567-3035
What It Contains: The center provides assistance/support to
                           small businesses, entrepreneurs and inven-
                           tors through technology transfer, including
                           technical and business feasibility studies.

Name of Resource: Technology Commercialization Program
Where To Find It: University of Illinois at Chicago
                           PO Box 4348, M/C 345
                           Chicago, IL 60680
                           (312) 996-9131
Who Could Use It: High-tech and manufacturing-oriented
                           companies—mostly beyond start-up stage
What It Contains: This program commercializes new ideas/
                           products and promotes technology trans-
                           fer in the fields of biotechnology, robotics,
                           mechanical devices, engineering software
                           and data processing hardware components.
                           It arranges assistance for qualified clients
                           in the areas of testing, prototyping, demon-
                           stration, market surveys and business plan-
                           ning. Staff and students are trained on the
                           latest, state-of-the-art applications.
Why Use It: When you need specialized research and
                           technical assistance and advanced train-
                           ing in highly technical environments

Name of Resource:	Technology Innovation Center
Where To Find It:	Northwestern University
	1840 Oak Ave.
	Evanston, IL 60201
	(708) 866-1818
	FAX (312) 491-4486
Who Could Use It:	Most businesses developing a product
What It Contains:	The center matches university resources with the needs of state business. It develops small business innovation research programs, links businesses to share technologies, develops international technology cooperatives, commercializes university technology and provides business planning activities for entrepreneurs. Research includes entrepreneurship, technology transfer, technology commercialization, economic development and business strategy. The center sponsors conferences and collaborates with the federal government of Thailand, the United States Agency for International Development and the International Business Development Program on Entrepreneurship in Thailand.

Another Similar Center

Name of Resource:	University of Chicago Technology Development Office
Where To Find It:	970 E. 58th St.
	Chicago, IL 60637
	(312) 996-4995

Incubators

Incubators are centers created to help businesses during their early stages. Incubators provide space at below market cost, as well as shared secretarial and bookkeeping services, and are referral sources for financing and general consulting. Some centers are designed to address the needs of specialized businesses, like the Evanston Incubator that focuses on high technology. For more information, contact:

The Evanston Business Investment, Corp. SBDC
Business Incubator
1840 Oak Ave.
Evanston, IL 60201
(708) 864-0800

Another popular incubator in the Chicagoland area is:

The Industrial Council of Northwest Chicago
Chicago Incubator at Fulton-Carroll Center for Industry
2023 W. Carroll Ave.
Chicago, IL 60612
(312) 421-3941

We hope that the incubator concept will continue to grow in this area. It provides younger businesses a safe place to nurture themselves long enough to become viable. Because resources are shared, so is the financial risk.

Additional information about incubators is available from:

National Business Incubation Association (NBIA)
One President St.
Athens, OH 45701
(614) 593-4331

NBIA lobbies on behalf of the incubator concept. Benefits of association membership include: the *Directory of Business Incubators*, a variety of helpful publications and annual conferences.

■ Resources _____

Special Assistance Centers for Women, Minorities and Family Businesses

Name of Resource:	American Woman's Economic Development Corporation (AWED)
Where To Find It:	(800) 222-AWED 10:00 A.M. to 5:00 P.M. EST
Who Could Use It:	Any entrepreneur/small business person
What It Contains:	For $5, this nonprofit organization offers a ten-minute phone consultation and quick answers to urgent business questions. Longer consultations (1 to 1 1/2 hours), $25
Why Use It:	To get quick definitive answers to specific business problems

Name of Resource: Chicago North Minority Business Development Center

Where To Find It: 1 Prudential Plaza, Ste. 700
Chicago, IL 60601
(312) 856-0200

Who Could Use It: Minority businesses

What It Contains: Business assistance for minorities

Why Use It: Free, general assistance

Name of Resource: Loyola University Chicago Family Business Center

Where To Find It: PO Box 257608
Chicago, IL 60625-7608
(312) 604-5005
FAX (312) 604-5094

Who Could Use It: Any business concerned with issues relative to family-owned businesses

What It Contains: This business center offers ongoing resources, a newsletter, annual public forums, library collection, research conducted on issues concerning family-owned businesses. A nonmembership organization and resource, the mission of this think tank is to further understanding, growth and development of responsible family-owned businesses in the Chicagoland area.

The Family Business Center supports research, hosts annual public forums on family business, conducts a membership program for a small group of sizable family businesses and publishes a newsletter as a service to the community of business owners and their families. It is in the process of developing an extensive library of family business-related materials.

Name of Resource: Offices of Women's Business Ownership
U.S. Small Business Administration

Where To Find It: 1441 L St., N.W., Rm. 414
Washington, DC 20416
(202) 205-6600

What It Contains: Programs for women business owners

Name of Resource:	Women's Business Development Center (WBDC)
Where To Find It:	8 S. Michigan Ave., Ste. 400 Chicago, IL 60603 (312) 853-3477
Who Could Use It:	Women or men
What It Contains:	The center provides entrepreneurial training and consulting in management, marketing, strategic planning, recordkeeping and other accounting and financial services, as well as business plan help. Additional programs include: Exchange groups, Women's Business Enterprise Initiative for women seeking opportunities in business and government, and The Women's Capital Fund that provides loans from banks and technical assistance from the center. Free counseling and training are available, and seminars on specialized topics are conducted on a regular basis. The center also organizes roundtable support groups for women business owners.
Why Use It:	Low-cost assistance; a good networking tool; cited by the United States Department of Commerce as one of the most effective and comprehensive technical assistance programs in the country.
When To Use It:	At start-up or expansion stage, specifically for women—when interested in obtaining government contracts.
Name of Resource:	Women's Work Force Network of Wider Opportunities for Women (WOW) and National Commission on Working Women
Where To Find It:	1325 G St., N.W., Lower Level Washington, DC 20005 (202) 638-3143
What It Contains:	This advisory board consisting of 500 community-based members throughout the country identifies and promotes broad-based opportunities for women.
Why Use It:	Has a small business development focus

General Educational Resources

Entrepreneurial programs are being developed at a rapid pace due to the increased interest in small business education. We suggest that you contact your local college for further information on available classes. Following is a partial listing of colleges that offer special programs for entrepreneurs:

■ Resources _____

Name of Resource:	Business and Professional Institute (BPI) and Small Business Development Center
Where To Find It:	College of DuPage 22nd St. and Lambert Rd. Glen Ellyn, IL 60137 (708) 858-2800 ext. 2592 (708) 858-2800 ext. 2771
What It Contains:	A variety of classes is offered, including business law, marketing and finance. Small Business Management 221, for example, deals with the details of planning and running a small business. Business assistance services and customized, on-site training programs are provided. Conferences, seminars, credit and noncredit courses, procurement assistance, technology transfer, employee outplacement services and professional continuing education units are organized for responsive delivery. Within BPI, the Economic Development Center (EDC) serves as a rich source of business training programs and services for the business community. EDC houses the Small Business Development Center, International Business Development Center, Conference Services Center, Procurement Assistance Center and Technology Commercialization Center.
Name of Resource:	Elgin Community College
Where To Find It:	Business Conference Center 1700 Spartan Dr. Elgin, IL 60123 (708) 697-1000 ext. 7321

What It Contains: Continuous/ongoing seminars are directed to the specific needs of small businesses. The recently developed 11-session Entrepreneurial Certificate Training Program contains integrated business development modules that cover everything from business planning to marketing and finance.

Name of Resource: Office of Continuing Education
Where To Find It: Chicago State University
                               95th St. & King Dr.
                               Chicago, IL 60628
                               (312) 995-2545

What It Contains: Mature students are offered career-updating and business-related courses, seminars and workshops for degree or nondegree credit, or noncredit status. Course work in advanced business, management, human relations and small business management, is provided in addition to on-site training and development for employees of small businesses involved in computer operation, budgeting, marketing and personnel management. Other courses are offered by the College of Business Administration.

Name of Resource: Office of Continuing Education
Where To Find It: William Rainey Harper College
                               Registration
                               1200 W. Algonquin Rd.
                               Palatine, IL 60067
                               (708) 397-3000

What It Contains: A variety of noncredit classes catering to the needs of the entrepreneur is available to anyone interested in starting a business. Classes such as "Selling Services" and "Importing and Exporting" are currently very much in demand.

Name of Resource: Small Business Entrepreneurship Program
Where To Find It: Oakton Community College/MONNACEP
1600 E. Golf Rd.
Des Plaines, IL 60016
(708) 673-4036
What It Contains: Start-up, management, marketing, accounting, financing and human resources courses are offered at locations in Des Plaines, Skokie, Park Ridge, Glenview, Northbrook and Evanston. It is possible to earn a certificate in Small Business Management.

■ Ten ■

Networking

■

Networking is critical to the success of your business, offering you the contacts and inside information you need to keep your pulse on the market. A frequently misunderstood skill, networking demands give and take. Unless the process is mutually beneficial, it helps no one.

The Benefits

Only you can determine what groups to join. Set your priorities. Your business commitments will not allow you enough time to get involved with the many available membership opportunities. Avoid spreading yourself too thin—start by joining one or two organizations.

If you take your membership seriously and get actively involved, you will benefit from participation in a professional or community organization. This is where others can see you in action. Ideally, participation in a combination of professional and general business organizations is beneficial. The best networks are those that make things happen by bringing regional and national issues to the community level. Such organizations actively promote their members and are therefore selective about whom they accept as members.

Thoroughly check out the programs and benefits offered by each organization you consider joining. Many organizations offer you an opportunity to get acquainted at business "after hours" meetings. There is usually no cost to attend these events, and you may even get some business. You will also want to attend several of each group's organizational meetings. Look for an affiliation that will increase your potential sources of business and provide you with opportunities to enhance and challenge your current expertise.

Meanwhile, collect lists from membership rosters, chambers of commerce and alumni directories. Start contacting these people to introduce yourself. Participate in at least one membership group, fund raiser, benefit or charity event yearly. Get involved in planning and organizing major meetings/celebrations. Always do this with complete dedication and attention to detail.

Attend breakfasts, luncheons, seminars and forums. The economic development breakfasts offered at the College of DuPage and at Harper College, for example, offer continental breakfast, a speaker's presentation on topics of interest to community businesses and an excellent opportunity to network.

General Networking Tips

- Join and participate regularly in community organizations and professional, technical or trade associations.
- Read and listen. Newsletters, professional and trade journals and magazines spur creative ideas and keep you aware of what's happening.
- Attend workshops, seminars and courses in your field, or explore new and related fields. Begin by contacting the continuing education department at your local college or university and professional, technical or trade associations.
- Use the telephone. Call to say "hello," to get an opinion or just to share some news.
- Schedule breakfast, lunch or dinner dates with peers.
- Invite others to visit your office, and arrange to visit theirs.
- Meet with a peer group on a regular basis.

- Affiliate or form other joint business relationships. Drawing on the contacts you make, set up joint projects with people in your field.

Networking Through Trade Associations

One of the best ways to meet people in business is through trade associations. In these organizations, industry professionals meet, share information and develop new business opportunities. Many trade associations publish newsletters and magazines that will help you stay abreast of the current state of your industry. Regular meetings present the opportunity to learn while establishing contacts. For a comprehensive listing of associations, check the *Encyclopedia of Associations* at your local library.

National Business Associations

There are many national associations that can be of benefit to your business. Those lacking local chapters can still provide you with opportunities to network with professionals in other parts of the United States. Contacting other business owners long distance can be an invaluable networking tool. These professionals are often invaluable sources of information about successful marketing strategies and sales techniques. Another benefit is that these long-distance telephone conversations tend to be short and concise. The individual on the other end of the line is usually flattered that you took the time to call long distance and therefore answers your questions as quickly and precisely as possible.

We recommend regularly keeping in touch with your long-distance business network. These professionals can become great sources for new information, as well as new business in the future. Long-distance networking can be extremely advantageous for business owners that have a national or international market potential. Following is a partial list of national associations you might be interested in joining:

■ Resources _____

Name of Resource:	American Economic Development Council
Where To Find It:	9801 W. Higgins Rd., Ste. 540
	Rosemont, IL 60018
	(708) 692-9944

What It Contains:	A national organization of professional economic and industrial developers publishes a monthly career opportunity newsletter.
Name of Resource:	American Entrepreneurs Association
Where To Find It:	2392 Morse Ave.
	Irvine, CA 92714
	(714) 261-2393; or for *Entrepreneur* magazine or a catalog of books and resources for the entrepreneur, call (800) 352-7449
What It Contains:	This association conducts in-depth research on new small businesses, sponsors seminars and publishes *Entrepreneur* magazine.
Why Use It:	Another resource for market research and general business development
Name of Resource:	Association of Black Women Entrepreneurs
Where To Find It:	PO Box 49368
	Los Angeles, CA 90049
	(213) 660-6248
Who Could Use It:	Female minorities
What It Contains:	Includes national networking, training programs and an SOS number for questions or concerns about business ownership. Membership includes ABWE's bimonthly newsletter that features resource information concerning contract information, trends and business tips. Membership also includes two free newsletter ads. Student mentors get support from ABWE members.
Why Use It:	Excellent resource for support/information
When To Use It:	Prior to, during and after start-up
Name of Resource:	Minority and Women-Owned Business Enterprise (MWBE) Program
Where To Find It:	AT&T Supplier Relations, MWBE Program
	PO Box 25000
	Greensboro, NC 24720
	(800) 322-MWBE
Who Could Use It:	Any female and/or minority owning at least 51 percent of their business who can supply goods and services from manufacturing to office equipment to information systems.

What It Contains: Every year the program focuses on finding a variety of new AT&T suppliers. The company is looking for businesses that can "see the total picture to provide customers the best technology, quality, service and price."

Why Use It: To obtain an opportunity to competitively bid to become a supplier of goods and services for AT&T

When To Use It: When you are capable of delivering the types of services or products AT&T is currently seeking

Name of Resource: National Association for the Self-Employed

Where To Find It: National Headquarters
2121 Precinct Line Rd.
Hurst, TX 76054
(800) 232-6273—General Information on Association
(800) 558-0043—Insurance Information

What It Contains: More than 145 membership benefits include discounts on car rentals, computer software, travel, long distance phone services. Consultant services, booklets on starting, evaluating and operating a small business, tax-saving tips for small business owners and much more. This is a major resource for group health, medical, dental and other insurance plans for the self-employed. A toll-free hotline—*Shop Talk 800* is available, as are advocacy and a newspaper published six times annually to update members on new developments affecting small business. Membership dues are $48/year.

Why Use It: A resource for cost-efficient operation of your business

Name of Resource: National Association of Women Business Owners (NAWBO)

Where To Find It: 600 S. Federal, Ste. 400
Chicago, IL 60605
(312) 922-0465

What It Contains:	This is the Chicago chapter of a national organization founded to provide guidance, information and referrals to women business owners.
Name of Resource:	National Association of Women Business Owners (NAWBO)—local chapter
Where To Find It:	825 Green Bay Rd., Ste. 270 Wilmette, IL 60091 (708) 256-1563 or (800) 238-2233
What It Contains:	NAWBO features monthly meetings, educational seminars and workshops, advocacy, certification and contract procurement assistance, an educational scholarship program and *Update*, a bimonthly news summary.
	Ask for a free packet containing information on NAWBO and its resources: Networking, training, communications, global activities, public policy, impact, corporate and political appointments and direct discount programs.
Why Use It:	This is a very strong group of business owners who can improve the quality of your business operations.
Name of Resource:	National Federation of Independent Business
Where To Find It:	600 Maryland Ave., S.W., Ste. 700 Washington, DC 20024 (202) 554-9000
Who Could Use It:	Any independent business person
What It Contains:	NFIB lobbies Congress on small business issues and provides information to entrepreneurs on regulations, legislation and federal agencies. Counselors troubleshoot business problems. Caseworkers intervene with federal agencies on members' behalfs
Name of Resource:	National Small Business United
Where To Find It:	1155 15th St., N.W., #710 Washington, DC 20005 (202) 293-8830
What It Contains:	NSBU represents 50,000 small businesses in its congressional lobbying efforts.

Benefits include a monthly newsletter, special conferences and seminars. Also, the organization will refer members to regional organizations for management assistance, seminars and networking.

■

Associations for Home-Based Businesses

Home-based entrepreneurs have a special motivation for networking. Although the range of businesses they represent is diverse, these entrepreneurs share many common concerns. Working alone, home-based professionals often crave the social contact that networking can provide.

■ Resources _____

Name of Resource:	National Alliance of Home-Based Businesswomen
Where To Find It:	PO Box 95
	Norwood, NJ 07648
	PO Box 306
	Midland Park, NJ 07432
	(201) 423-9131
Who Could Use It:	Any home-based business
What It Contains:	This organization provides assistance with matters and issues pertinent to businesses operating from residential homes as well as two excellent publications, *Planning for Home-Based Businesses* and *Zoning for Home-Based Businesses*.
Name of Resource:	National Association for the Cottage Industry
Where To Find It:	PO Box 14460
	Chicago, IL 60614
	(312) 472-8116
Who Could Use It:	Anyone interested in home-based businesses or cottage industries
What It Contains:	A support network for home-based businesses and cottage industries that publishes a

quarterly newsletter, *The Cottage Connection*, for $45 a year.

Why Use It: To stay abreast of and network with this segment of the market

Name of Resource: National Association of Home-Based Businesses

Where To Find It: PO Box 362
Owings Mills, MD 21117
(410) 363-3698

What It Contains: This association helps connect media with home business owners for free national and local publicity. Members receive special offers created exclusively for them. Free membership: Send business card, home business name and address and additional descriptive business information.

Name of Resource: Work-at-Home Special Interest Group

Where To Find It: Compu-Serve Information Service
(800) 848-8990

Who Could Use It: Any business

What It Contains: You can take an "electronic coffee break," attend a conference or ask for guidance about working from home, all without leaving your desk.

Cooperatives

A cooperative is a business owned and controlled by the people using it—producers, consumers or workers with similar needs who pool their resource for mutual gain. Members have an equal voice in cooperative matters; they invest in shares to provide operating capital and assure that their businesses provide high-quality products and services at the lowest possible cost. Today, 100 million Americans belong to 45,000 cooperatives that range in size from small buying clubs to businesses included in the Fortune 500. They include:

- Mutual insurance companies
- Credit unions

- Agricultural marketing and supply cooperatives
- Rural electric and telephone cooperatives
- Consumer goods and services cooperatives
- Small business cooperatives
- Health, child care, housing and telecommunications cooperatives

Familiar cooperatives include: The Associated Press, Florist Transworld Delivery (FTD), Ocean Spray, Land O'Lakes, Nationwide Insurance, Sunkist, Group Health, Inc. and Ace Hardware.

Founded in 1961 and known for many years as the Cooperative League of the USA, the National Cooperative Business Association (NCBA) is a national membership and trade association representing America's 45,000 cooperative businesses and their 100 million workers.

The National Cooperative Business Association
1401 New York Ave., N.W., Ste. #1100
Washington, DC 20005
(202) 638-6222

NCBA provides assistance in the development of cooperatives and represents its members before Congress and the federal agencies. It also promotes and supports cooperative businesses through training and technical assistance programs, journals and the sale and distribution of cooperative resource materials.

■ Resources _____

Other Professional Associations For Family Business Owners

Name of Resource:	Chicago Family Business Council, Inc.
Where To Find It:	401 N. Michigan Ave., Ste. 2600
	Chicago, IL 60611
	(312) 245-1760
What It Contains:	Support for the family-owned business
Name of Resource:	National Family Business Council
Where To Find It:	1640 W. Kennedy Rd.
	Lake Forest, IL 60045
	(708) 295-1040
What It Contains:	The council holds monthly meetings and publishes a newsletter.

For Consultants

Name of Resource:	Consultant's National Resource Center
Where To Find It:	PO Box 430
	Clear Spring, MD 21722
	(301) 791-9332
What It Contains:	Membership is free to consultants. For more than ten years, the center has been providing consultants with publications like *Consulting Opportunities Journal*. It also has an extensive catalog of books, periodicals, software and other resources for consultants and small business owners.

Name of Resource:	Society of Professional Business Consultants
Where To Find It:	8 S. Michigan Ave.
	Chicago, IL 60603
	(312) 922-6222

For Women Business Owners

Name Of Resource:	Chicago Association of Women Business Owners
Where To Find It:	600 S. Federal St., Ste. 400
	Chicago, IL 60605
	(312) 922-6222
What It Contains:	This national network group of women owning their own businesses holds monthly meetings, conducts seminars and publishes a newsletter.

Name of Resource:	Chicago Commission for Women
Where To Find It:	510 N. Peshtigo Ct., 6A
	Chicago, IL 60611
	(312) 744-4427
What It Contains:	Managers and advocates to improve the status of women in the Chicago area

Name of Resource:	Chicago Women in Trades
Where To Find It:	37 S. Ashland
	Chicago, IL 60607
	(312) 942-1444
Who Could Use It:	Women working in the skilled trades— construction and manufacturing fields as electricians, machinists, carpenters, auto

What It Contains:	mechanics, pipefitters, ironworkers, painters, laborers, firefighters and more—are welcome. Membership is also open to women who seek to enter the trades and who support the goals of the organization. This organization educates its membership on job rights, skill building, safety concerns and other issues relevant to tradeswomen. Job and apprenticeship openings are publicized through the Job Hotline, and a pre-apprenticeship tutorial program is available to prepare women for entry into skilled trades. Monthly meetings.

Name of Resource:	National Association for Women in Careers
Where To Find It:	Northwest Suburban Chapter
	PO Box 72275
	Roselle, IL 60172
	(708) 934-5299
What It Contains:	This association features networking, newsletters, monthly workshops, membership directories and speakers for all women interested in a mutually supportive environment and the ability to integrate and balance career growth and private life.
Why Use It:	For personal development and to establish a networking system for continued growth
When To Use It:	Before, during and after business start-up

Name of Resource:	National Network of Women in Sales
Where To Find It:	West Chapter—(708) 462-5255
Who Could Use It:	Any entrepreneur, particularly those devoted to sales-based businesses
What It Contains:	Education, support, promotion, networking, social interaction with peers, national job bank and monthly seminars are available.

Name of Resource:	Office of Women's Business Ownership
Where To Find It:	U.S. Small Business Administration
	409 Third St., S.W., 6th Fl.
	Washington, DC 20416
	(202) 205-6673

What It Contains:	Regularly offers programs of interest to women business owners
Name of Resource:	North Suburban Network of Women Entrepreneurs
Where To Find It:	PO Box 298 Winnetka, IL 60093 (708) 835-8911
What It Contains:	A group of noncompeting women entrepreneurs who meet regularly to exchange business leads
Name of Resource:	Women's Professional Sales Network
Where To Find It:	825 Green Bay Rd., Ste. 270 Winnetka, IL 60091 (708) 256-0264
What It Contains:	A professional women's group for networking and educational opportunites. The group holds monthly breakfast and dinner meetings. Each meeting has a speaker addressing a sales-related topic, including motivational areas.

■

Local Business Associations

Not all associations are tied to a specific industry. Small businesses may organize regionally or along common interests that transcend industry boundaries.

■ Resources _____

Name of Resource:	DeKalb County Economic Development Corporation
Where To Find It:	(815) 895-2711
What It Contains:	This resource provides location factors and operations-related data, quality of life-related information, census and demographic information, statistics concerning employment, industry performance and wages, salaries and benefits.

Why Use It:	This corporation offers business advocacy, a directory, networking, financing assistance with banks and state, counselors, seminars, managerial advice, library resources, business development, federal procurement assistance, technology and product development.
Name of Resource:	DuPage Area Association of Business and Industry
Where To Find It:	(708) 469-8088
Who Could Use It:	All business people in DuPage county
What It Contains:	Information resources are available concerning the area, quality of life, census and demographics, economic and labor projections for the county.
Why Use It:	Business advocacy directory, networking, newsletter
Name of Resource:	Illinois Manufacturers' Association
Where To Find It:	(312) 922-6575
Who Could Use It:	Any manufacturing business
What It Contains:	This local industry association offers a variety of conferences throughout the year
Name of Resource:	Illinois Small Business Association
Where To Find It:	18200 Sherman St. Lansing, IL 60438 (708) 895-7700
What It Contains:	This voluntary organization provides goods/services to consumers and a voice for independent Illinois business persons in manufacturing, services, distribution, farming, the professions, construction and property rental.
	The group promotes the interests of small business and serves as a resource for governmental and regulatory issues.
Why Use It:	For help with issues and filing procedures as related to taxes, minimum wage and overtime laws, management assistance, sales procurement, new laws including OSHA, EPA, EEOC, Wage and Hour, "Consumer" agencies and much more.

Name of Resource:	The Inventors and Entrepreneurs Society of Indiana (TIES)
Where To Find It:	PO Box 2224
	Hammond, IN 46323
	(219) 989-2354
What It Contains:	We have listed this Indiana group because we believe it can be of benefit to Chicago area entrepreneurs. It has a great collection of exciting people doing exciting things. The group, which meets monthly, is a place where people who are creating products can find resources to get them into the market and make money. This group is chartered by the state of Indiana as an educational resource.
Who Could Use It:	Inventors, consultants, attorneys

Chambers of Commerce

Chambers of Commerce support investment within their communities and are excellent sources of local business news, advice and support, demographic/economic data, special seminars and programs for small businesses, and representation of the business community before government entities. Chambers may also provide statistics on such factors as market characteristics, the labor force, local facilities, transportation and traffic that can help in business location decisions. Additionally, many chambers now offer leads groups.

■ Resources

Name of Resource:	Chicagoland Chamber of Commerce
Where To Find It:	200 N. LaSalle St., Ste. 600
	Chicago, IL 60601
	(312) 580-6900
Who Could Use It:	Any business within the Chicago metropolitan area
What It Contains:	This is the Chamber of Commerce for all of Metropolitan Chicago. It offers seminars

on a broad range of personnel and training topics for small businesses and works closely with the United States SBA and the state of Illinois to provide comprehensive support for smaller companies.

Name of Resource: Chicago Southland Chamber of Commerce
Where To Find It: 1154 Ridge Rd.
                          PO Box 1698
                          Homewood, IL 60430
                          (708) 957-6950
What It Contains: A regional chamber serving the 69 south suburbs, Southland offers a wide variety of networking opportunities.

Other Chambers of Commerce in the Chicago area include:

Albany Park Chamber of
Commerce
4745 N. Kedzie Ave.
Chicago, IL 60625
(312) 478-0202

Arlington Heights Chamber
of Commerce
215 N. Arlington Heights Rd.
Arlington Heights, IL 60004
(708) 253-1703

Barrington Area Chamber of
Commerce
325 N. Hough St.
Barrington, IL 60010
(708) 381-2525

Bloomingdale Chamber of
Commerce
113 Fairfield Way, #301 D
Bloomingdale, IL 60108
(708) 980-9082

Brighton Park Business
Association
4363 S. Archer Ave.
Chicago, IL 60632
(312) 376-4880

Calumet Area Industrial
Commission
1000 E. 111th St.
Chicago, IL 60628
(312) 928-6000

Chicago Lawn Chamber of
Commerce
6013 S. Keating
Chicago, IL 60629
(312) 585-6227

Continental Africa Chamber
of Commerce
One N. LaSalle St., Ste. 2450
Chicago, IL 60602
(312) 782-8859

East Side Chamber of Commerce
3658 E. 106th St.
Chicago, IL 60617
(312) 721-7948

Edgebrook Chamber of
Commerce
5318 W. Devon
Chicago, IL 60646
(312) 775-0378

Elgin Chamber of Commerce
24 E. Chicago St.
Elgin, IL 60120
(708) 741-5660

Elmhurst Chamber of Commerce
& Industry
105 Maple Ave.
PO Box 752
Elmhurst, IL 60126
(708) 834-6060

Greater O'Hare Chamber of
Commerce (GOA)
1050 Busse Rd., Ste. 100
Bensenville, IL 60106
(708) 350-2944
A regional chamber, primarily
for Elk Grove, Bensenville,
Itasca and Wood Dale

Hoffman Estates Chamber of
Commerce
2400 W. Central Rd.
Hoffman Estates, IL 60196
(708) 765-9300

Hyde Park Chamber of
Commerce
1765 E. 55th St.
Chicago, IL 60615
(312) 288-0124

Jefferson Park Chamber of
Commerce
4651 N. Milwaukee Ave.
Chicago, IL 60630
(312) 545-5635

Lincoln Park Chamber of
Commerce
1323 W. Diversey Pkwy.
Chicago, IL 60614
(312) 880-5200

Mont Clare-Elmwood Park
Chamber of Commerce
14 Conti Pkwy.
Elmwood Park, IL 60635
(708) 456-8000

Mount Greenwood Chamber
of Commerce
3101 W. 111th St.
Chicago, IL 60655
(312) 238-6103

95th Street-Beverly Hills
Business Association
9006 S. Hoyne Ave.
Chicago, IL 60620
(312) 238-4094

Northwest Association of
Commerce and Industry (NSACI)
Zurich Towers II
1450 E. American Ln., Ste. 140
Schaumburg, IL 60173
(708) 517-7110
A regional chamber; one of
the largest in the country

Portage Park Chamber of
Commerce
4921 W. Irving Park Rd.
Chicago, IL 60641
(312) 777-2020

Rogers Park Chamber of
Commerce
7001 N. Clark St.
Chicago, IL 60626
(312) 764-8000

Roselle Chamber of Commerce
102 S. Prospect
Roselle, IL 60172
(708) 894-3010

Streamwood Chamber of
Commerce
PO Box 7028
Streamwood, IL 60107-7028
(708) 837-5200

Uptown Chamber of Commerce
4743 N. Broadway
Chicago, IL 60640
(312) 878-1184

Wheeling/Prospect Heights
Area Chamber of Commerce
and Industry
395 E. Dundee Rd., Ste. 300
Wheeling, IL 60090
(708) 541-0170

■ Resources

Name of Resource:	Corridor Group
Where To Find It:	3033 Ogden Ave., #203
	Lisle, IL 60532
	(708) 769-0885 or (708) 682-6005
What It Contains:	This association of public relations and communications professionals representing companies engaged in high technology and research and development activities offers *The Economic Development Guide,* an updated source of information and contacts for businesses and associations in this four-county area. Additionally, this group offers a newsletter, workshops, seminars, meetings, breakfast exchanges and luncheon meetings and visits to sites along the Illinois Research and Development Corridor. (This corridor, also known as the I-88 Corridor, extends from Oakbrook in DuPage Country through DeKalb, Kane and Kendall counties.)

Why Use It:	An excellent resource for contacts and business in the Illinois Research and Development Corridor
Name of Resource:	Golden Corridor
Where To Find It:	William Rainey Harper College 1200 W. Algonquin Rd. Palatine, IL 60067 (708) 537-5420
Who Could Use It:	Those interested in economic development
What It Contains:	This regional marketing organization undergirds the economic development activities of its members.
	The Opportunity newsletter is funded in part by the Illinois Department of Commerce and Community Affairs Opportunity Program.
Why Use It:	Networking/working with others in the community to build stronger business climates

Leads Organizations.

The idea behind leads groups is to assemble a limited group of members, each representing a different business category. The intent is to exchange business leads with one another in an effort to bring more business to members. Chicago has a number of leads opportunities. Dues for the groups vary: Some are relatively inexpensive, while others can run more than $1,000 per year. If the expense is too high, or you have trouble finding a group that has an opening, consider forming a group yourself.

Most newspapers have special calendar sections for business organizational news. If you are forming a nonprofit group, you can put your meeting news in these sections. Call your local paper, ask for the calendar editor and find out the deadline for listing information. Newspaper listings can generate new members *and* new business opportunities. Following is a partial list of area leads clubs. Check your chamber of commerce; they often have leads groups for members.

■ Resources

Name of Resource:	Association of Networking Women
Where To Find It:	(708) 665-7523 or (708) 858-0558
What It Contains:	This small networking group, which meets the third Tuesday of each month, limits membership to one business per business classification.

Name of Resource:	E.X.E.L. Network, Inc.
Where To Find It:	PO Box 1102
	Lombard, IL 60148
	(708) 627-5647
Who Could Use It:	Women who wish to develop and expand their businesses
What It Contains:	This is a support network and direct referral system dedicated to career progress, financial advancement and personal growth.
Why Use It:	To develop a mutually beneficial network for support and referrals

Name of Resource:	Leads Club
Where To Find It:	(815) 436-5495
What It Contains:	A networking group for men and women with membership limited to one business in each business classification. The group meets every Thursday at 7:30 A.M. to share leads and information.

Name of Resource:	Women Entrepreneurs of DuPage County
Where To Find It:	616 Enterprise Dr.
	Oak Brook, IL 60521
	(708) 572-3230
Who Could Use It:	Any woman entrepreneur in DuPage County who has 50 percent or more interest in a partnership or corporation or who owns her own business.
What It Contains:	Workshops, seminars, breakfast and luncheon meetings, newsletter, educational programs, business development opportunities, limited membership by occupation
Why Use It:	Networking and educational benefits

Mentors

Contrary to popular belief, you never outgrow your need for a mentor. Mentors are vital for support, reassurance and advice. They serve as tools for career and business advancement and are as helpful to the older, growing business as to the start-up.

Be careful. Choose a mentor not because you like him or her but because this is a person who can challenge you. Keep your antennae up once you know what you need in a mentor. Chemistry helps, but the relationship will not spring forth full-blown without some effort. Trust takes time. Be sincerely interested in your mentor's business and progress—quality mentoring should be a two-way street. Remember that mentorships—like any relationship—can change and fade away. It is important to keep yourself open to new mentor relationships.

Places to start looking for a mentor who would understand the needs of an older business include the Young Presidents Organization, (212) 867-1900 and the Chicagoland Enterprise Center, (312) 427-7773.

The Mentoring Program offered by the Chicagoland Enterprise Center, is targeted at companies with committed management interested in creating or retaining jobs in the Chicago metropolitan area. Companies that meet these requirements can tap into a strong network of consultants who work on a volunteer basis in the areas of market analysis and planning, operating plan development, quality control procedures, cost control systems, management skills development, business and strategic planning and general information. Mentors commit to meeting with clients on a regular basis for a full year to provide feedback and advice. The center also serves as a clearinghouse for information on local nonprofit and government-sponsored economic development organizations.

Check with the National Association of Women Business Owners (NAWBO) at (312) 922-6222 or (800) 238-2233. Ask for Joyce Knauff who works with the older business owner. She is currently creating an Information Exchange group for women who have been in business more than seven years and is spearheading the creation of the Destiny Institute Mentoring Program.

You might also look for an entrepreneurial consultant. If you do, find someone who specializes in working with businesses such as yours, and who is capable of challenging you. You don't need someone to hold your hand, but you do need someone who has the insight to help you bring your goals into clearer focus.

Expos, Conferences, Workshops and Seminars

Read local newspaper listings and trade magazines to learn about special programs that could be networking opportunities.

■ Resources _____

Name of Resource:	Annual Entrepreneurial Woman's Conference and Annual Women's Business and Buyers' Mart
Where To Find It:	Sponsored by the Women's Business Development Center Hyatt Regency Chicago Hotel Call The Womens Business Development Center, (312) 853-3477
What It Contains:	An opportunity to meet a variety of contract procurement corporations
Name of Resource:	Annual World Trade Week Seminar and Exposition Sponsored by the International Trade Association, DePaul University and the United States Department of Commerce
Where To Find It:	(708) 980-4109
Name of Resource:	Chicago Small Business Expo
Where To Find It:	Chicago ExpoCenter 350 N. Orleans Chicago, IL 60654 Call the Chicagoland Chamber of Commerce at (312) 580-6928, for more information.
What It Contains:	Sponsored by The Chicagoland Chamber of Commerce, U.S. Small Business Administration, Illinois Department of Commerce

& Community Affairs and the City of Chicago (Department of Economic Development, and Department of Purchases, Contracts and Supplies)

Usually held in November, the Expo showcases small business goods and services as a means for local companies to gain exposure for their products. Informative educational sessions and individualized counseling services are available.

Name of Resource:	Entrepreneurial Woman's Conference VI
Where To Find It:	Women's Business & Buyers Mart
	Hyatt Regency
	Chicago, IL 60601
	Sponsored by Women's Business Development Center
	(312) 853-3477
What It Contains:	Usually held in the fall, t his is an opportunity to meet with a large number of companies who are interested in working with women.

Name of Resource:	Franchising for Women & Minorities
	The National Association of Female Executives and Women in Franchising
Where To Find It:	(800) 222-4943
	FAX (312) 431-1469
What It Contains:	Presented nationally by American Airlines (Usually held in mid-June)

Name of Resource:	Visions and Ventures
Where To Find It:	Triton College
	2000 N. Fifth Ave.
	River Grove, IL 60171
	(708) 456-0300 ext. 539
What It Contains:	Held in late spring/early summer, this conference provides professional development opportunities for women in business, and offers strategies for women business owners.

Be Open to Opportunities

Once again we will repeat the overriding message of this book: "Be informed." It's up to you to find opportunities and do your own networking. The best organizations will be those specific to your business and your needs. The benefits of networking cannot be emphasized enough. It is helpful just to find people with whom you can share your triumphs and your difficulties. Now with more and more business "outsourcing," networking is a great way to pick up business or spot joint venture opportunities.

■ Eleven ■

Managing Your Business

■

Whether you have established your business as a sole proprietorship, a partnership or a corporation, your management skills—or your ability to hire someone to provide those skills—will be critical to the success of your business. As an entrepreneur, your focus has been on conceiving, gathering resources, organizing and running your business. During the developmental phase of your business, you must take steps to form internal systems for managing so that your operations flow more smoothly. You will then have more time to do the things that really grow your company—like marketing and sales.

If you are a sole proprietor with full responsibility for all aspects of your business, you don't need to worry about human resources. But you do need to be skilled at managing time and energy levels and to balance the varied needs of your business—from production to collections. You will want to organize your office for the greatest efficiency and to tap into every possible high-tech tool that your budget will allow.

Successful business owner-managers are incredibly well-organized. They have developed keen conceptual skills that enable them to acquire, analyze and interpret information from various sources and then to make complex decisions. These entrepreneurs see the *big picture* and plan ahead rather than reacting to outside influences. Leaders who can inspire others with their vision, they learn to handle administrative tasks and budgeting. If they don't, they don't survive. To succeed, owner-managers develop the technical skills required to complete the tasks that keep their business functioning—or they find outside experts to help them.

Time Management

Time management, a subject written about extensively, is probably as important to the growing business as sales. Successful entrepreneurs have control over their time—it is the one skill that propels them forward at a consistent rate of growth. Thalia Poulos, president of Time Planners, Inc., a time management coaching and training firm in Chicago, comments, "I emphasize self-management over time management. Good self-management could save entrepreneurs as much as one hour a day. For service-based companies that are essentially selling their time, that extra hour can really make a difference—not only in sales, but in the personal development of the business owner."

Ms. Poulos adds that effective self-management is based in discipline. Entrepreneurs have a tendency to get trapped into taking on too much. They often overbook their appointments, their administrative tasks and even their networking opportunities. A better way to handle the many tasks required to build a business would be to first prioritize them as follows:

An "A" priority task—something that directly relates to achieving one of your goals For example, you want to start growing new business opportunities by giving talks at various clubs. The first step, then, might be to contact an organization such as Toastmasters to develop your speaking skills.

A "B" priority task—something that indirectly relates to achieving one of your goals These tasks don't carry as much of an immediate need to complete. The important element here is to make sure that these tasks are done *after* any "A" priority tasks. For example, reading a book on giving special presentations might be a "B" priority task.

An important thing to remember about time management or self-management is that priorities can change often, even daily. You must be flexible, allowing change when new opportunities arise. Instead of the traditional *To-Do List*, Ms. Poulos recommends using a *Do-It List* (**Do** Only **I**mportant **T**hings). Many business owners feel as though they are always busy, working long hours but not necessarily accomplishing what they wanted to do. Poulos refers to this experience as "the barrenness of business taking over." Being "goal-minded" together with "time-minded" is the key to getting out of this time trap.

There are many scheduling and organizing tools on the market, some of them quite expensive. There is no way to recommend one over another because every business and every person have particular needs and styles. Be sure that the system you choose is easy to maintain and does what you want it to do.

Delegation

The fine art of delegation is an extremely important skill for you to learn regardless of whether you manage a business with several employees or just manage yourself. No one can function effectively alone; those who attempt to do so fall prey to burnout. Although delegation can be a difficult process for anyone accustomed to keeping tight controls over their business operations, it can greatly improve efficiency.

The best way to strengthen a small business is to delegate to outside experts. Consider asking a banker, an accountant, a management consultant, an attorney or another local business owner to serve on an informal board of directors. A monthly meeting of such a board can yield good advice and become an ongoing source of business development. The group can also be used as a sounding board for future business decisions.

You'll find that you can delegate and still keep control if you follow some very simple guidelines:

1) Let go of responsibilities for tasks that do not address your top priority.
2) Know exactly what your goals are, and then make sure they are measurable and specific. Prioritize expectations.
3) If you have an overload of work, find someone—perhaps even a competitor—and subcontract small projects to them. Find someone who can deliver and doesn't cut corners. Consider training, ability and availability.
4) Establish reasonable checkpoints for communication between yourself and your subcontractor. Formalize a system ahead of time so that fellow professionals don't feel you are questioning their competence.
5) Consider delegating the entire project—based on the project's complexity and your subcontractor's competence. Listen to your subcontractor's expertise.
6) When a project goes sour, consider allowing the subcontractor to take responsibility and correct any problems he or she has caused. Patience in this area can lead to profitable long-term business relationships.
7) Have an agreement specifying the performance standards, budget, deadline controls and procedures for final review (when and how a formal review will be handled). Be free with your feedback—positive and negative. This enables subcontractors to know if they are on track.

Temporary Assistance

Long before you're ready to hire employees, you should prepare yourself in order to ensure that you will make well-educated choices when the time comes. Carefully evaluate the kind of individuals you need to bring into your organization. While working with other professionals and businesses, observe the kinds of skills and work tactics that mesh best with your own. Develop your ability to communicate your needs and motivate others to follow through.

You will need salespeople. Consider using outside reps who work on straight commission. This arrangement—typically an independent contractor relationship—allows flexibility on both sides. Your salespeople set their own hours and goals, and you pay them only when a sale is made.

You might also use independent contractors in other areas of your business. Many computer programmers, for example, work as independent contractors. All small businesses have special projects for which independent contractors are appropriate.

A word of caution is in order here. In the past, a number of small businesses falsely classified employees as independent contractors in order to avoid unemployment insurance, payroll taxes and social security payments. As a result, the IRS has targeted abuse of the independent contractor status for auditing. Penalties for noncompliance are severe—100 percent in the case of payroll taxes, and the owner's personal assets are liable. Carefully review federal, state and IRS regulations to be sure that any temporary help arrangement you set up conforms to the legal definition of the independent contractor. This is a confusing area of the law. If there is any question in your mind, we advise you to consult your attorney.

Another method for securing workers to fill gaps in your workload is to tap into the temporary job market. Temporary workers fill a very definite need. They work on a per job basis for a day, a month or a year, and they are not on your payroll. You hire temporary workers from a service, which is responsible for tax liabilities. You benefit in another way—you have help when and where you need it without paying an individual for *down time* when business is slack.

Don't be put off by the idea of temporary workers. Today's temp agencies offer workers with many different levels of skill and expertise—everything from bookkeepers to computer consultants. Some agencies specialize in secretarial help, while others can provide you with technical, financial or managerial personnel. Temp services offer skilled, prescreened workers, and they frequently offer the option of permanent placement. Be sure to check with the agency's policies concerning permanent placement of temporary personnel in the event that you decide you would like to offer a temporary worker a permanent job.

These aren't the only resources you can tap into when seeking qualified talent. In addition to advertising in newspapers, try your own trade and association newsletters and magazines. Solicit referrals from business acquaintances, organizations and friends. Check with other associations, particularly secretarial and computer users groups. Post a note on electronic bulletin boards. Approach universities and technical/vocational schools—most of them offer job assistance programs.

Temporary services cannot fill job orders for home-based offices. If this is a problem, think about hiring individuals outside the standard temp job market. Chicago is filled with professionals willing to work on an on-call basis to earn extra money.

Permanent Employees

You may want to start planning for permanent employees with an ongoing search. Collect the resumés of those who impress you, and categorize them according to the role they could one day fill in the development of your business. Conduct information gathering interviews. Exploratory interviews serve the purpose of qualifying the interest of the individuals in possible future alliances. Explain your interest and intent; ask these professionals to keep you apprised of their progress. Those who continue to update you and show promise stand out as the best candidates for your company when the need arises.

If you expect to do much hiring, you may want to contact the Society of Human Resource Professionals, (312) 368-0188.

As you develop a reputation as a solid business owner, you will also be able to network with business leaders in your community—even if they are outside your own industry. If you're looking for someone to fill a top spot in electronics, don't pass up the chance to discuss your credentials and employment needs with the recruiting executive of an advertising firm. He or she just might have the hidden connection that could lead to the talent you need. Network with recruiters from many industries, both related to your own business and others. It's the only way to learn about available talent.

Employees are your company's lifeblood and most valuable resource. You will generally get back as much, or more, from them as you are willing to invest. Consider investing in their continued education and upgrading of skills, and capitalize on every opportunity to foster their abilities. Employees given a sense of pride and co-responsibility will contribute much to the growth of your business. You might want to consider cross-training your employees so that they are well-versed in all facets of your business and capable of performing multiple tasks within your organization. Common wisdom today is to seek out those people who know how to function without organizational charts— people who are able and willing to make decisions and take responsibility for the outcome.

While you are looking for workshops, seminars and other educational opportunities for yourself, you might also keep an eye on what is available for employees. Also consider subscribing to newsletters and magazines that are focused on updating employee skills.

Employee Manual

Before hiring anyone permanently, you should have an employee manual in place that complies with all IRS and OSHA requirements. The handbook, which is not intended as an employee contract, should be updated regularly. When setting up your employee handbook you might want to include many of the following topics to avoid misunderstanding and conflicts later:

- Introduction of the company and company policies
- Company history and financial status
- Working hours and sign-in procedures
- Rest periods/coffee breaks
- Rules for absences
- Pay periods
- Safety and accident-prevention programs
- Policies on phone usage
- Vacations and holidays
- Compliance with the American Disabilities Act and similar regulations/laws
- Policy on jury duty and military leave
- Employees' rights to unemployment compensation
- Medical, hospital and surgical benefits
- Pensions, profit sharing and bonuses
- Group insurance
- Training programs
- Parking rules
- Service awards
- Credit unions

When To Hire a Manager

There is no best time to hire an outside manager. However, you need to recognize that there comes a time when hands-on attention to the details of growing and operating a business reaches a point of negative return.

Sometimes entrepreneurs find that the investment of more time and energy fails to produce a comparable return. Simply put, your growing business may require more expertise than you have. It is then that you must decide whether to bring in new managerial help or to curtail continued growth.

When you bring in an outside manager, you must give up control. Managers are an important part of business growth. It is best to bring in new managers when the business is on course and holding steady with increasing profits—after the start-up period is completed. Bringing in that outside manager frees you up to conquer new worlds. Before the search begins, you must consider compensation. A good resource is the *Executive Compensation Booklet* from Price Waterhouse. This 19-page booklet on executive compensation packages, includes information on phantom stock, deferred performance bonuses and stock appreciation rights. You can order by calling (212) 819-5000.

Employee Benefits

Insurance is the most critical benefit question facing small business today, and clearly there are no easy answers. Although few small businesses can afford costly benefit packages, there are other ways to compete against larger companies for employees. Take advantage of your flexibility. Listen to the needs of your employees. Sometimes all it takes is a small concession like flexible working hours to make an employee happy; and the small business is better able to respond to that type of need.

You should talk to your accountant about creative compensation packages that will help keep valued employees. High-tech companies have used stock options quite successfully in gaining the commitment of key employees. Look into profit-sharing or retirement savings plans that are financially within your reach.

In Chapter 3 we focused primarily on property and casualty insurance; here we are addressing the need small business owners eventually have for health-care insurance. A recent article in *Inc.* magazine stated that insurance premiums have been on the rise—by as much as 25 percent yearly. The article also reported that many insurance companies refuse to provide coverage for small businesses. And although there is legislation pending that would help curb the rise of insurance costs, there is no question that there is still much work to be done in the area of small business medical insurance programs.

Perhaps, the best advice we can give you is to take time to shop for coverage using all the resources available. For example, many chambers of commerce and trade and professional associations offer special group plans. See Chapter 10 for specific names of chambers and associations that might provide such plans. A good resource is the National Association for the Self-Employed.

Once you have found a good medical plan, consider picking up a part of the premium and having your employees pay the balance. In a special issue of *Home Office Computing* (January, 1992), author Linda Stern gave this advice, "Forget about buying an expensive, top-quality health insurance policy. It simply doesn't exist. At best, you'll find a reliable, solid policy that fits your needs at a cost you can afford."

The first thing you want to look for is whether the insurance company you are considering has a proven record of safety and reliability. You probably don't have the time to evaluate the performance of more than 2,500 insurance companies on your own, so you will need to rely on an impartial third-party resource such as A.M. Best Company, Standard & Poor's Corporation or Moody's Investors Services.

Best has been recognized as a leading firm in analyzing the financial strength of insurance companies since 1899. Ratings are based on what Best thinks of a company's relative strength and operating performance.

Standard & Poor's has been rating companies since 1923, and rating the Claims-Paying Ability of insurance companies since 1971. Moody's Investors Services originated a system of rating securities in 1909. This system was first applied to insurance company policyholder obligations in 1986. Moody's considers all phases of the life insurance industry when assigning ratings.

Another good source of information is other business owners who already have policies. Ask them what they like and don't like about their current policies. Make a prioritized list of the services you value the most, and compare these services with the features offered in available policies.

Publications

There are literally hundreds of good books about managing in today's business climate. Your best bet is to browse the bookstore shelves and pick out a few books that suit your needs. Listed below are SBA publications on management issues. Call the Illinois Business Hotline (800) 252-2923 to order:

Business Continuation Planning   An overview is provided of business owner's life insurance needs that are not typically considered until after the death of one of the business's principal owners.

Business Life Insurance   Prepared by the Institute of Life Insurance. U.S. Small Business Administration Office of Business Development, Management Aid, Number 2.009. SBA, PO Box 15434, Fort Worth, TX 76119. The phone number is (817) 334-3777.

Buying for Retail Stores   The latest trends in retail buying are discussed. The book also includes a bibliography that references a wide variety of private and public sources of information on most aspects of retail buying.

Checklist for Developing a Training Program   A step-by-step process for developing an effective employee training program is outlined.

Choosing a Retail Location   Learn about current retail site selection techniques such as demographics and traffic analyses. This publication addresses the hard questions the retailer must answer before making the choice of a store location.

Effective Business Communications   The importance of business communications and how they play a valuable role in business success is explained.

Employee Benefits (publication) and *Employee Benefits Analyzer* (computer program), U.S. Chamber of Commerce, (800) 638-6582. The publication offers a comprehensive reference guide for employers and benefits specialists; the interactive computer program is designed to perform comparative benefits analyses.

Employees: How To Find and Pay Them   A business is only as good as the people in it. Learn how to find and hire the right employees.

Fixing Production Mistakes   Structured as a checklist, this publication emphasizes the steps that should be taken by a manufacturer when a production mistake has been found.

How To Buy or Sell a Business   Learn several of the techniques used in determining the best price to buy or sell a small business.

How To Get Started with a Small Business Computer   This publication helps you forecast your computer needs, evaluate the alternative choices and select the right computer system for your business.

Insurance Checklist for Small Business   Mark R. Greene, U.S. Small Business Administration, Office of Business Development, Management Aide #2.018, PO Box 15434, Fort Worth, TX 76119. The phone number is (817) 334-3777.

Inventory Management   Purposes of inventory management, inventory types, record keeping and forecasting inventory levels are discussed.

Is the Independent Sales Agent for You?   This book provides guidelines that help the owner of a small company determine if a sales agent is needed and pointers on how to choose one.

Locating or Relocating Your Business   Learn how a company's market, available labor force, transportation and raw materials are affected when selecting a business location.

Managing Employee Benefits   Employee benefits are described as one part of the total compensation package. The proper management of benefits is discussed.

OSHA Handbook for Small Businesses, #2209   For a single free copy, send a self-addressed, stamped envelope to: OSHA Publications Office, Room N-3101, U.S. Department of Labor, Washington, DC, 20201. The first in a safety management series to inform employees of voluntary protection and compliance programs. It includes information on: employee involvement, management commitment, work site analysis, hazard prevention and control, training for employees, supervisors and managers. A comprehensive, updated, self-inspection checklist provides the framework for identifying hazards in the work place. The booklet also provides information on the availability of a free OSHA consultation for employers.

"People: Managing Your Most Important Asset," *Harvard Business Review*.   Soldiers Field, Boston, MA 02163; phone (800) 274-3214. Brief scholarly reports on various aspects of dealing with communication issues within and without the business environment.

Problems in Managing a Family-Owned Business   Specific problems exist when attempting to make a family-owned business successful. This publication suggests how to overcome these difficulties.

Purchasing for Owners of Small Plants   An outline of an effective purchasing program is presented, as well as a bibliography for further research into industrial purchasing.

Should You Lease or Buy Equipment?   Various aspects of the lease/buy decision are described. It lists advantages and disadvantages of leasing and provides a format for comparing the costs of the two.

Small Business Decision Making   This will help you acquaint yourself with a wealth of information available on management approaches to identify, analyze and solve business problems.

Small Business Risk Management Guide   Strengthen your insurance program by identifying, minimizing and eliminating business risks. This guide can help you secure adequate insurance protection for your company.

Starting a Retail Travel Agency   Travel agencies are a rewarding yet challenging business. Learn how to start one.

Techniques for Problem Solving   The key techniques of problem solving and problem identification are presented for the small business person, as well as a design for implementing a plan to correct these problems.

Techniques for Productivity Improvement   Learn to increase worker output through motivating "quality of work life" concepts and tailoring benefits to meet the needs of your employees.

"301 Great Management Ideas," *Inc. Magazine*   (800) 372-0018 ext. 4182 Information is included about cost control, benefits, employee relations and more. Topics include: how to eliminate the problem of "no-shows" with hourly employees, how to save thousands of dollars on the cost of your company medical insurance, and a sure-fire program for getting rid of your accounts receivable bad debt.

■ Resources _____

Name of Resource:	American Management Association (AMA)
Where To Find It:	135 W. 50th St.
	New York, NY 10020
	(800) 262-6969
What It Contains:	The association provides those who manage current information on management practices and techniques. Ask for a free *Catalog of Seminars*, which offers diverse courses for managers. Members are also entitled to free and unlimited use of AMA's management information and library service and to attend regional briefings by leading experts and receive discounts on

all AMA courses including Padgett-Thompson, Keye Productivity Center, Success Builders and The Business Women's Training Institute courses.

Name of Resource:
Where To Find It:

The Business Exchange
5 Revere Dr., Ste. 200
Northbrook, IL 60062
(800) 551-0622

What It Contains:

This service is for both small-sized and mid-sized companies. It offers CEOs the opportunity to meet 10 times a year with a group of up to 15 noncompeting businesses. An experienced moderator leads the groups through specific problem-solving exercises. According to one of the group's partners, "The new ideas produced by the group help the CEO lead his or her firm to work smarter, to increase sales and improve profits." Running a company can be a lonely undertaking, since there is no one person who can appreciate all the challenges a CEO faces—except another CEO. Joining The Executive Committee gives company leaders a unique forum for support and learning.

Name of Resource:

The Executive Committee (TEC) and The Business Exchange, Ltd. Headquartered in San Diego, CA.

Where To Find It:

Call (703) 953-1473 or (312) 477-0390 for information.

What It Contains:

Membership is by invitation with qualifying criteria: company must gross at least $2 million per year and have at least 25 employees. TEC groups in Chicago, consisting of 7 to 14 chief executives, meet one day a month; their goal is to help one another be more effective in running their businesses. These organizations are part of a nationwide network. Professional resource speakers with strong backgrounds in business consultation can be an excellent resource for the smaller business. Here, they get the latest advice from prominent business experts, and share with one another the problems and opportunities that arise in their companies. Each CEO's group meets for a full day once a month.

Name of Resource: **Where To Find It:**	Insurance Information Institute 110 William St. New York, NY 10038 (212) 669-9200 Toll-free business and consumer hotline: (800) 331-9146
What It Contains:	The institute offers help minimizing costs and maximizing protection on your business and/or personal insurance. The staff will confer with you over the phone, or send you free publications.

Name of Resource: **Where To Find It:**	Inter-Pay 505 E. Golf Rd., Ste. C Arlington Heights, IL 60005 (708) 228-9077
What It Contains:	Inter-Pay provides a company with instant payroll computing. There is one monthly fee for the processing, which includes payroll management reports.

Name of Resource:	National Association of Professional Organizers
Where To Find It:	1163 Shermer Rd. Northbrook, IL 60062 (708) 272-0135
What It Contains:	This professional organization for time management specialists provides regular meetings and operates as a resource to those looking for assistance in this area.

■ Twelve ■

The Growing Business

■

This book was written and researched with you in mind. It is your spirit that inspired us to construct a resource guide designed to help the Chicago small business community grow and prosper. We have personally experienced the peaks and valleys of small business ownership, and we've learned a few lessons along the way. You are the beneficiaries of those lessons. The *Sourcebook* has been constructed to put financing, marketing, legal, personnel, business plan and organizational contacts at your fingertips.

We're believers in the adage, "Success is a journey, not a destination." And, so, let us move together into the future. In this chapter we will assume that you have weathered a few years of business ownership. Initially you were fighting alligators, focusing on survival instincts. By now you are probably experiencing growing pains and gains. Your administrative and accounting systems should be in place. Your business identity should be gaining recognition. You, and everyone you work with, should know what your product is, who your target market is, what price ranges you function in and how you get your message and product out to that targeted market. You should have a pool of satisfied customers and a track record of dependability and profitability. If you find that your business is lacking in any of these areas, look back at prior chapters to determine exactly what you need to do to bring your company up to speed.

Unless you were one of the fortunate few able to obtain a start-up loan, you may now be thinking of taking out a loan to sustain the growth of your business. We urge you to think this through very carefully. A business that is successful frequently finds that it can continue to develop and grow at a respectable speed without obtaining financing.

We have hypothetically separated the new and the older business at this three-year point because the three-year track record seems to be what lenders look at when evaluating a business's viability. However, three is not a number cast in stone. You may have reached this maturity much sooner, particularly if you had a strong financial base going in or if you had solid managerial skills. On the other hand, you may still be floundering a bit—getting the kinks out of your business and reaching solid financial ground.

Eventually, you will be ready to evaluate where you are and what your next stage of development will include. Not all businesses want to become mega-corps with hundreds of employees. In fact, current wisdom stresses a preference toward downsizing—staying small for optimum market flexibility Make your plans cautiously, they will determine the direction your business will grow.

Beware the Pitfalls

At the three year point you may begin to feel the need to change—to do something different. Often a major overhaul in image, marketing procedures, location or even business status (whether to continue or to try a new venture) is decided upon. This is also where you run the highest risk of burnout.

Many entrepreneurs instinctively know when they have come to a fork in the road and that major decisions need to be made to continue growing. These professionals come to the realization that they can no longer reach their maximum potential by working harder or faster. At the same time, entrepreneurs need to remember that any change needs to be a logical outgrowth of what has gone before.

Now it's time to start working smarter, using the knowledge and skills accumulated throughout the start-up period and drawing on a history of successes with customers. This is where you need to redouble your use of the information resources available to you.

How Strong Is Your Business—Really?

The first area of your business that needs to be carefully evaluated is your budget. A budget does more than control spending. It helps anticipate expenses and enables you to plan ahead for purchases such as equipment, advertising, extra staff, etc., that your company will need. The budget also should help make financial uncertainty more manageable.

By now you have experienced the natural peaks and valleys of your business. You know, for example, that you can expect a substantial increase in business before Christmas but that February is generally a slow month.

A quick examination of last year's budget can help you determine your annual cost of doing business. Identify the fixed costs you have some control over and which ones are outside of your control. Are your numbers realistic? Is there any waste that can be trimmed?

Evaluate the kind of reasonable profits you can expect in the next year. Set a goal, but make it realistic. Profit projections should be achievable—making you stretch and grow without being oppressive. You might set goals for each product or service line or each individual in your organization to determine how each contributes to the profitability of the whole. If you're offering a product or service line that is eating up your profit margins, you should consider doing away with it.

Look at your budget as a flexible tool. It is not an end in itself and should not be cumbersome or overly time-consuming. Because it is based on future expectations and is meant to serve as a map, you can deviate from your budget as long as you remember your goal—to stay *within* your projections.

There are no universal numbers or formulas that fit all businesses. Check your company ratios against average ratios for businesses similar to your own. These can be obtained through your trade associations, trade magazines or the annual reports of similar companies. The numbers might be different, but using the ratios, you should be able to create a good analysis of important financial ratios for your business. Accountants, financial consultants and bank loan officers can also help you determine the key ratios for your business. Some basic formulas you will want to be familiar with because they allow you to determine the health of your company include the following:

- *Current Ratio*   The measure of your company's solvency is one of your most critical assessments. This is the ratio revealed on your company's balance sheet. All assets (including cash, inventory, accounts receivable) are divided by all current liabilities (property taxes, payroll, loan payments). You'll want to keep your ratios in line with the industry if you hope to obtain a loan.

- *Gross Profit Ratio*   This ratio is determined by subtracting cost of goods sold (including raw materials, direct labor and overhead) from the gross sales. The answer is your gross profit. Now divide the gross profit by the gross sales. How does this percentage compare with the ratios of similar companies in your field or industry? If your gross profit ratio is not on target, you need to look at what's going on. Your first inclination may be to increase prices. But it's also possible that you are losing money on excessive administrative costs, or other expenses.

- *Return On Investment (ROI)*   This calculation, figured by taking net profit (gross sales minus all costs including taxes) as a percentage of invested capital, will tell you whether your company yields an acceptable return and warrants further investment. When the ROI is less than the percentage your money could be earning in a money market account or other passive investment, you will want to consider whether cutting costs or diversification of products is called for, or whether you should simply sell out and invest in a more lucrative venture.

■ *Inventory/Turnover Ratio* This ratio would be important if your company maintains an inventory. Your goal is to keep your inventory costs low and your turnover high, running your company with as little inventory as possible without limiting sales opportunities.

When analyzing your company to determine bottom line, cash flow and profits, the numbers to use are not the dollars but rather the important relationships between various components of your business. Only you can determine what those key components are and what the ratios for maintenance of your business's health should be, but consider the following possibilities:

■ When your main expense is people: Revenues divided by number of employees will tell you that you need to do something soon if your financial ratios drop.
■ Client or job numbers should generate a known stream of revenues and expenses. If productivity figures decline or costs get out of line with the ratio model, look at expenses as a percentage of revenues.
■ Consider setting net revenue as the denominator, and check the ratios with cost categories to determine the percentage of net revenue.

If you now have more staff and service more customers, or take on more projects, the dollars should be there (if you are pricing your product or service high enough). You should also know how much income each customer brings in and how much in the way of costs that income justifies—all through examination of ratios.

Risk, Growth and Planning

With the knowledge and expertise of several years behind you, you are now capable of taking more calculated risks. You can try new tactics based on probable outcomes. This is a good time to sit down with a management consultant to discuss your new growth stage and the opportunities and risks associated with it. When you do so, you should have a firm idea of where you are and where you want to go.

You developed a business plan when first starting your business. If you haven't been using it regularly to create monthly or even yearly action plans, it's now time to look at it again. Updating this plan will keep you on target and propel you to the next plateau of small business growth. It will also demonstrate to potential lenders, if you choose to take this route, that you are indeed on top of a viable business.

Short-term goals should consist of plans for the next year. Long-term goals will include perhaps three-year, five-year and ten-year projections. Remember, however, one of your greatest strengths as a small business person is that you can move quickly to meet unforeseen changes in the economic environment and the market. Your plan must be adaptable as needed for changing conditions in the marketplace.

Moving beyond survival, you need to provide strong organizational leadership and long-range vision for yourself and your business. Somewhere between the inception of your business and the point where it will reach peak development, you need to make some serious decisions.

Do you want to diversify and expand your business, offering new products, services, hiring more employees, entering new markets? Maybe, maybe not, depending on the long-range goals you set. At every plateau in the growth of your business, there are trade-offs. For every change you make in your operations and structure, there will be ramifications that you need to be prepared for. For example, if you decide that you have been working alone long enough and now want to take on employees, you don't just hire a new person to work with you. Will an employee produce enough to justify the payroll cost? You need to restructure your accounting processes, rethink your IRS requirements and realign your workload—perhaps delegating more and taking on new managerial roles.

Many business owners avoid planning. They think planning limits their flexibility, is impossible in an uncertain business climate or takes too much time away from day-to-day business. Marion Foote, a specialist in strategic financial management for small businesses, offers several reasons for creating a plan for your business:

- *Flexibility*   Planning expands your options. If you do not know where you're going, you often end up somewhere you didn't intend to go. When you know where you want to go, you can decide how to get there. Then, if you run into a roadblock, you can find a new route to your destination.
- *Change*   Planning reduces uncertainty and helps you share ideas with your associates. To operate in a changing environment, you need everyone's talents and ideas to find the best route through the changes affecting your business.
- *Time*   Studies show that small-sized to medium-sized businesses currently spend four to ten days per year on the planning process—less than five percent of annual working time. This is a small price to pay for one of your most valuable assets—a map for success.
- *Direction*   As you develop plans for the business, you share your goals and objectives with the people who can help you reach them. A shared understanding of where you're going helps everyone work toward the same goal.

Credit and Credit Management Resources

As a growing business, you probably have found that cash flow is increasingly important. You may have a large number of new accounts, but you have to hire new employees to start servicing those accounts. These new internal expenses are often temporarily greater than your receivables. Knowing what you can and cannot do with regard to extending credit to customers is crucial to the growth of your business.

The Dictionary of Business and Credit Terms defines credit as "the ability of an individual or business enterprise to obtain economic value on faith, in return for an expected payment of economic value in the future. Credit management is the executive function of skillfully planning, organizing and supervising the credit policies of a company."

Businesses large and small can benefit from credit management services that offer credit reporting, collection services and a variety of credit management programs. The following three resources are listed to help you address these needs:

■ Resources

Name of Resource:	The Chicago-Midwest Credit Management Association
Where To Find It:	315 S. Northwest Hwy. Park Ridge, IL 60068 (708) 696-3000 FAX (708) 696-1372
What It Contains:	Founded in 1896, this organization exists to educate members in credit management and to provide a full range of credit management services that include: credit reporting services; industry credit groups; meetings and education; collection services; management services; and adjustment services.

Membership benefits include: immediate access to their national database of business credit information; monthly scheduled seminars and workshops; assistance with staffing for credit departments; use of their progressive collection program; assistance when involved with financially distressed businesses; and a quarterly newsletter subscription.

Name of Resource:	Dun & Bradstreet Credit Services
Where To Find It:	Dun & Bradstreet, Inc. 299 Park Ave. New York, NY 10171-0074 (212) 593-6800
What It Contains:	A resource for credit reports for small-sized to mid-sized companies

Name of Resource:	TRW Business Credit Services
Where To Find It:	505 City Pkwy. W., Ste. 100 Orange, CA 92668 (714) 991-6000
What It Contains:	TRW offers a variety of small business education and information services in addition to standard credit reporting services. Send for an information package. Networking is provided between co-ops (like

businesses nationally and internationally). Members can apply for technical assistance anywhere in the world.

--- ■

Partnering

Partnering is one of the hottest business concepts of the 1990s. You can partner by entering into long-range relationships with other related, compatible businesses that might be serving the same end user. You can develop cooperative projects with competitors so that each might profit. Or you can look for opportunities to work with a larger company—or marketing rep companies—to act as their preferred or exclusive supplier.

In theory, partnering allows a smaller company the opportunity to create strategic alliances that can result in more business. However, there are advantages and disadvantages. The advantages are obvious: increased revenues, decreased marketing costs, long-term investments based on future sales volume, and more efficient planning with an increased ability to plan purchases and production schedules. The disadvantages, although fewer in number, must be carefully considered. They include an increased risk if the other company decides to end the relationship, a tendency to become dependent on one large partner and often unwelcome demands upon your development schedule.

Weigh your options before agreeing to such a relationship. Reduce your risk by becoming and staying attuned to your market. Knowing the inner workings of your market can help you anticipate market changes that can affect your relationship. Don't rely on just one business relationship for more than 30 percent of your business. This way, if even unforeseen circumstances result in the loss of a relationship, you can downsize moderately while looking for the next opportunity. As with your personal well-being, it is balance that is required.

Contract Procurement—Opportunities for More Business

The federal government buys everything from shoelaces to soap. You could find a ready source of business here, since the government sets aside a number of procurement opportunities for small businesses. Be forewarned, however, that it can take some real work on your part to isolate which one of the over 4,500 government agencies might be in the market for your services.

If you are interested in bidding on contract opportunities with the state of Illinois, take a look at *The Lincoln Courier* (217) 732-2101, the state's official daily newspaper. *The Courier* provides information on all state bids and contract opportunities, including information on who to contact and how to respond to Requests for Proposals (RFPs), etc.

There are also small business development centers that offer assistance with contract procurement. See Chapter 9 to locate a center near you. Other sources of assistance include firms that specialize in contract bidding like Rome and Associates or Contract Bidding Consultants, Inc., both located in Chicago.

Karen Banning of Contract Bidding Consultants recommends focusing on one market at a time. She reports that generally, profit margins with government contracts are not as high as those in the commercial markets. But higher volume and guaranteed receivables make government contracting an attractive *business building* technique and an excellent business education source.

■ Resources

Name of Resource:	Business Service Center of GSA
Where To Find It:	Federal Information Center
	(800) 366-2998
Who Could Use It:	Anyone seeking bidding opportunities with the government
What It Contains:	This is the source for invitations for bids with the government. Call the Federal Information Center, which will direct you to the appropriate federal government office.
Why Use It:	To get on a list for solicitations for bids

Name of Resource:	*Commerce Business Daily*
Where To Find It:	Superintendent of Documents
	U.S. Government Printing Office
	Washington, DC 20402
	(202) 783-3238 or (202) 377-0633
	—or the public library—

What It Contains:	This national booklet contains a daily list of all proposed procurements of $25,000 or more by civil and military agencies of the Federal Government. It also contains lists of contract awards, announcements of surplus property for sale and foreign business opportunities.
Why Use It:	To stay abreast of bids let out by the government and solicitations
When To Use It:	Any time you pursue this area of business

Name of Resource:	Defense Department
Where To Find It:	Regional Office Chicago Contact the Federal Information Center (800) 366-2998
Who Could Use It:	Anyone who wishes to secure bids with the Defense Department
What It Contains:	A resource for bids
Why Use It:	To bid on contracts

Note: The SBA helps groups to band together to bid on government contracts and provides names of prime government contractors. Subcontracting qualifies you for SBA assistance.

Name of Resource:	Dialog-File 195
Where To Find It:	Dialog Information Services, Inc. (415) 858-3810
What It Contains:	*Commerce Business Daily* is updated daily (the evening before the version becomes available). Each procurement record in the database contains an abstract describing the item/service desired, whom to contact, estimated price range and if the contract has been set aside for small businesses.
	All information is completely searchable. You can request specific Requests for Proposals (RFPs), Requests for Quotations (RFQs) and Invitations for Bids (IFBs), and they will be ready whenever you sign on. This is a government database.
Who Could Use It:	Anyone
Why Use It:	Easy access to a ready source of business

Name of Resource:	Federal Business Service Center
Where To Find It:	230 S. Dearborn St., Rm. 3714
	Chicago, IL 60604-1503
	(312) 353-5383
Who Could Use It:	Any business interested in offering services to the federal government
What It Contains:	The Federal Business Service Center offers counseling on GSA and government contracts for established businesses. It also is a resource for current publications on specific business topics.

A wealth of information is available as a result of research and information sharing via federal channels. *Consumer Information Catalog* includes timely and helpful publications from almost every agency of the federal government.

Consumer Information Center has a small staff of consumer information specialists available on a selected basis to speak at or participate in national conferences.

Why Use It:	To identify opportunities for doing business with the government and to locate information on your individual business

This is a valuable up-to-date resource for a variety of topics—particularly from the federal information perspective—and a guide in many areas of business.

Name of Resource:	General Services Administration—U.S. Federal Government Procurement Office
Where To Find It:	(312) 353-5395 or (800) 424-5210
	—or—
	General Services Administration, Region 5
	230 S. Dearborn St.
	Chicago, IL 60604-1503
	(312) 353-5383
Who Could Use It:	Anyone seeking to do business on a bid or contract basis with the federal government and its agencies

What It Contains:	GSA provides expert advice and a *Federal Procurement Directory.* Information is available concerning regional bidding opportunities; subcontracting opportunities; contracting for new or improved items; referrals to other federal buying activities; federal specifications for bidding purposes; general federal procurement and the *National GSA Forecast,* regarding minority and women-owned business programs.
Why Use It:	To locate bid and contract opportunities and to obtain appropriate forms.
When To Use It:	When ready to start doing business with the Federal Government and its agencies
Name of Resource:	Rome and Associates, Ltd.
Where To Find It:	175 W. Jackson Blvd., Ste. 1629 Chicago, IL 60604 (312) 922-2248
What It Contains:	These government contract advisors provide complete bid preparation and monitoring opportunities through negotiation and financing.

Publications

Doing Business with the Federal Government and *Women Business Owners: Selling to the Federal Government,* U.S. Government Printing Office, Superintendent of Documents, (415) 858-3810. Valuable information concerning requirements of form and format required in preparation for your response to a request for proposal (RFP) or other procurement notices.

Exporting

As we become more and more globally oriented, exporting opens up new horizons for small business. Although most companies currently exporting are product-based, service-based businesses can also find new customers overseas. Once again, it takes some time and legwork.

For the most part the resources listed are those offered by the federal government. However, there are other resources offered by the state and nongovernmental agencies. We emphasize government resources because they are very useful and inexpensive. They offer a great opportunity to gain knowledge of new business opportunities with little or no financial risk. Refer to the list in Chapter 9 of small business development centers offering International Trade Centers. These centers can help you: determine whether exporting is right for you; evaluate your company's export potential; develop your international trade business plan; and explain how to use an export management company or an export trade company to increase your international sales. They can also help you:

- Obtain export financing, and explain how to use it to increase your export sales;
- Understand export licensing;
- Understand the cultural aspects of international trade; and
- Promote and advertise your product in other countries.

■ Resources _____

Name of Resource:	American Association of Exporters and Importers
Where To Find It:	11 W. 42nd St. New York, NY 10036 (212) 944-2230
Who Could Use It:	Any business seeking expansion through export opportunities
What It Contains:	This trade association works to solve the problems of disseminating information to the international trade community. It takes legislative action on issues that impact exporters and importers, acts as an information clearing house on issues and provides publications that address the issues.
Name of Resource:	Department of Economic Development
Where To Find It:	24 E. Congress Pkwy., Ste. 700 Chicago, IL 60605 (312) 747-7400

Who Could Use It:	Any business seeking export opportunities
What It Contains:	Assistance is available to Chicago firms looking for international export opportunities.

Name of Resource:	Executive Options, Ltd.
Where To Find It:	707 Skokie Blvd., Ste. 600
	Northbrook, IL 60062
	(708) 291-4322
Who Could Use It:	Women balancing careers, independent consultants and retired executives
What It Contains:	This group places professionals in permanent, part-time and project assignments. Entrepreneurs benefit from this service due to the flexible work arrangements and because they don't have to pay benefits.

Name of Resource:	Export Information System (XIS)
Where To Find It:	SBDC (sponsored by the SBA)
	Available through your local SBA, SCORE or SBDC office
What It Contains:	Developed by the International Trade Division at the University of Georgia, this is an import/export data bank of trade information containing approximately 2,500 product categories showing their performance in the world market. This information, from which trade reports are created, is based on the Standard International Trade Classification (SITC) statistics supplied by the United Nations. An XIS Report will provide specific product information on: (1) the top 35 importing countries, (2) United States exporters' top 25 world markets, based on percent of market share and dollar sales and volume and (3) market growth trends for the past five years.
Why Use It:	This is an excellent tool to help a start-up decide what kind of product or service to offer or for an existing business planning for future product or service development.

Name of Resource:	Export Opportunity Hotline
Where To Find It:	Small Business Foundation of America
	(800) 243-7232

Who Could Use It:	Any company interested in researching and approaching foreign markets
What It Contains:	Operators answer questions on foreign market research, export financing, licensing and insurance, documentation and finding assistance.
Why Use It:	An excellent free (except for some services) resource

Name of Resource:	Export Revolving Line of Credit Loan Program
Where To Find It:	The U.S. Small Business Administration (800) U ASK SBA
Who Could Use It:	Applicants must qualify as small businesses and be in business for at least one year.
What It Contains:	Designed for those businesses seeking short-term financing to sell their products and services abroad. The program guarantees repayment to a lender in the event of a default by an exporter.
Why Use It:	This program provides financing for the labor and materials needed for manufacturing, to purchase goods or services for export, to develop foreign markets or to finance foreign accounts receivable.

Name of Resource:	Industry and Trade Administration
Where To Find It:	Office of Public Affairs U.S. Dept. of Commerce Washington, DC 20230 (202) 377-2000
What It Contains:	Motivational films on exporting

Name of Resource:	International Trade Assistance
Where To Find It:	The U.S. Small Business Administration (SBA) (800) U ASK SBA
Who Could Use It:	Businesses with at least one year of operations who are interested in exporting
What It Contains:	Financial and business development assistance is available to help small businesses develop export markets.
Why Use It:	Expedites the exporting opportunity

When To Use It: Contact this office after you have been in business for 12 months and satisfy general requirements for obtaining SBA loans. This requirement may be waived if your company's management has sufficient export trade experience or enough management ability to warrant an exception.

Name of Resource: International Trade Club of Chicago
Where To Find It: 203 N. Wabash, Ste. 2208
Chicago, IL 60601
(312) 368-9197
What It Contains: A forum for communication on international opportunities, the group is comprised of attorneys, exporting manufacturers, international consultants and anyone else interested in international trade.

Name of Resource: International Trade Loan Program
Where To Find It: The U.S. Small Business Administration (SBA)
(800) 827-5722
Who Could Use It: Small businesses engaged or preparing to engage in international trade
What It Contains: Up to $1.25 million is available, less the amount of SBA's guaranteed portion of other loans outstanding to the borrower under the SBA's regular lending program. Proceeds may be used for working capital and/or facilities or equipment, including purchasing land and building(s).
Why Use It: This program helps small businesses that are engaged/preparing to engage in international trade, as well as small businesses adversely affected by competition from imports. Loans are made through lenders under the SBA's Guaranty Loan Program.
When To Use It: Those interested in developing export markets. Applicants must establish either that loan proceeds will significantly expand existing export markets or develop

new ones or that the applicant's business is adversely affected by import competition.

Name of Resource: Overseas Ventures/Export Financing
Where To Find It: Overseas Private Investment Corp.
1100 New York Ave., N.W.
Washington, DC 20527
(800) 424-6742 or (202) 457-7010
What It Contains: Contact for loans for export financing and overseas ventures
Who Could Use It: Companies seeking financing for exporting or overseas ventures

Name of Resource: Small Business Export Hotline
Where To Find It: (800) 243-7232
Who Could Use It: Anyone interested in international trade opportunities
What It Contains: You'll get the private-enterprise angle on international trade. Information is provided on export financing, what to expect from and how to deal with the Commerce Department, licensing and insurance requirements, distribution, language issues and developments in Eastern Europe.

Name of Resource: The U.S. Department of Commerce, Rm. 6043
Where To Find It: Washington, DC 20230
(202) 377-2645 or (202) 377-4473
Who Could Use It: Anyone interested in international trade
What It Contains: To take advantage of new markets in Eastern Europe, you need a lot of information from the United States government. Assistance in locating resources is provided. Call for publications, upcoming international events and referrals.

Name of Resource: Women in International Trade
180 N. LaSalle St., Ste. 2920
Chicago, IL 60601
(312) 641-1466
What It Contains: This group for management-level women who work in aspects of international trade

offers educational programs, speakers, newsletters and special events.

——————————————— ■

Publications

Business Book Review (708) 304-5550 or (800) 236-REVU   This quarterly publication, edited by reknown marketing consultant Jagdish Sheth, Ph.D., offers in-depth reviews of top business books.

Facts Delivered (800) 832-1234   Dow Jones Information Services, offers a reasonably priced clipping service for any kind of news you might want to monitor. Information is delivered via your fax on a monthly basis. Get the latest news and background on a prospect, investment, client or competitor.

Market Overseas with U.S. Government Help   The overseas marketplace offers exciting opportunities for increasing company sales and profits. Learn about the programs available to help small businesses break into exporting. Call (312) 353-5133 to order this booklet from the Federal Government Bookstore.

Newstrack (800) 525-8389   This bimonthly service puts 14 key summaries on tape from a library of over 100 business magazines.

Soundview Executive Book Summaries (800) 521-1227   This helpful service provides monthly summaries of current business books.

The Inner Strength of Successful Small Businesses

Do you remember the entrepreneurial survival skills we described in Chapter 1? By now they should be your credo.

Be ethical, even in hard times.

Know your customers' needs and satisfy them.

Take the time to do something extra for your customers.

Focus your energies on the bottom line.

Pay attention to accounts receivable.

Control your inventory.

Reduce expenses.

Minimize paperwork.

If you're an entrepreneur, you are a survivor. You constantly demonstrate to yourself and to others that you are in for the long haul. You exhibit a rare commitment to do whatever it takes to get the job done. You face struggles with your eyes wide open and have learned to turn problems into challenges and opportunities. You thrive on risk, challenge and accomplishment.

The entrepreneurial journey can at times be a lonely one. The resources contained in this book have been compiled to provide you with help along the way. We have walked the path you're walking. We know how it feels to strive, fall down, pick ourselves up and start all over again. We know the incredible thrill that accompanies success. We understand the addiction of the entrepreneurial challenge, and we wouldn't live our lives any other way.

Someday, perhaps we'll have the opportunity to do business together. In the meantime, here's to you, Chicago entrepreneurs. Talk about *big shoulders*!

■ Who We Are ■

We would be remiss if we didn't include ourselves as invaluable resources to Chicago area entrepreneurs. Melissa's company, The HAIMS Group, helps businesses grow and prosper.

Joan-Marie's company, J-M and Associates, is a full-service public relations firm.

■ Resources

Name of Resource: The HAIMS Group
Where To Find It: 1901 N. Roselle Rd., Ste. 500
Schaumburg, IL 60195
(708) 882-9913
(800) 93-HAIMS [(800)-934-2467]
What It Contains: Entrepreneurial Consultants who offer services to small businesses, assisting new and expanding businesses by providing a management team to supplement management, marketing, sales and technical needs until volume of sales is sufficient for permanent full-time replacement

Name of Resource: J-M and Associates
Where To Find It: 131 Fairlane Ct. B
Bloomingdale, IL 60108
(708) 980-8539
What It Contains: Public relations/desktop publishing with focus in publicity and newsletter production; offers production services, consultation and training workshops for in-house production

■ Appendix A ■

Office Resources— Equipment, Supplies, Furnishings

■

Following are just a few of the many office resources available to the entrepreneur. New businesses emerge every day to meet the ever increasing needs of small businesses, so this list is far from complete. Other sources we recommend include:

- *Newspapers* Try the classified section of your Sunday papers. They contain listings of businesses selling furniture and office equipment.
- *Garage Sales* Large tables make great desks. You can also find equipment like file cabinets and even used computers.
- *Word-of-Mouth* Put the word out at your local chamber of commerce or among friends. We've found several great buys from businesses willing to sell old equipment at a fraction of its original price.

■ Resources _____

Name of Resource:	Abbey Press
Where To Find It:	Hill Drive
	St. Meinrad, IN 47577
	(812) 357-8011
What It Contains:	A wonderful source of cards, posters, all-occasion notes and gifts that are perfect public relations supplies for entrepreneurs.

Name of Resource:	Able Furniture
Where To Find It:	80 N. State St.
	Elgin, IL 60120
	(708) 742-6550
What It Contains:	This five-story warehouse filled with new and used furniture for home and office is an excellent resource for inexpensive furniture.

Name of Resource:	A.J. Nystrom & Co.
Where To Find It:	3333 Elston Ave.
	Chicago, IL 60618
	(312) 463-1144
What It Contains:	A resource for maps, globes and atlases

Name of Resource:	At-Home Office Works
Where To Find It:	26 W. 225 Geneva Rd.
	Wheaton, IL 60187
	(708) 653-7899
What It Contains:	An extensive selection of products specifically for the home business from furniture, computers and faxes to supplies and services. Training seminars and equipment repair are also offered.

Name of Resource:	DAK Industries
Where To Find It:	8200 Remmet Ave.
	PO Box 7120
	Canoga Park, CA 91304-9955
	Customer Service: (800) 888-7808
	Orders: (800) 325-0800
What It Contains:	This is a catalog order resource for inexpensive electronic equipment that features free technical support and a price protection policy.

Name of Resource: CompUSA (The Computer Superstore)
Where To Find It: 1057 E. Golf Rd.
Schaumburg, IL 60173
(708) 619-0333 or (708) 619-1221
What It Contains: A warehouse of values in computer hardware and software

Name of Resource: Office Max
Where To Find It: Numerous locations throughout the Chicago metropolitan area
What It Contains: Substantial discounts on a variety of supplies and furnishings for businesses and schools

Name of Resource: Quill Office Products
Where To Find It: 100 Schelter Rd.
Lincolnshire, IL 60069-3621

PO Box 4700
Lincolnshire, IL 60197-4700
(708) 634-4800
What It Contains: A resource for inexpensive office supplies, equipment and furnishings

Several payment options are available: 30-day open accounts, Visa or Master Card charges, easy monthly payment plan on some major purchases. Rapid turnaround is featured, and shipping is free on orders of $45 or more.

Name of Resource: Quill Office Furniture & Clearance Center
Where To Find It: 701 N. Rt. 53
Itasca, IL 60143-1348
(708) 773-1110
What It Contains: A wide selection of in-stock office furnishings (e.g., partitions, computer furniture).
Why Use It: Substantial savings of up to 65 percent off manufacturers' list prices when furnishing your office

Name of Resource: Sam's Club
Where To Find It: New warehouses are opening all the time such as those located in:
Alsip (708) 385-7597

Cicero (708) 863-2593
Evergreen Park (708) 422-7532
Gurnee (708) 885-1130
Matteson (708) 747-7979
Naperville (708) 527-0880
Northlake (708) 531-0807
Streamwood (708) 213-8622
Wheeling (708) 541-9040

Who Could Use It: Anyone who owns, operates or manages a business

What It Contains: This is a members-only warehouse outlet of quality merchandise at substantial savings. Verification of business status, consisting of two forms of identification, is required.

Name of Resource: The Signery

Where To Find It: 100 E. Roosevelt Rd.
Villa Park, IL 60181
(708) 530-4411

What It Contains: An extensive selection of interior and exterior signs for businesses

■ Appendix B ■

How Long Should You Keep Business Records?

■

One Year

Correspondence (unimportant) with customers and vendors
Duplicate deposit slips
Purchase orders (except purchasing department copy)
Requisitions
Stockroom withdrawal forms

Three Years

Bank deposit slips
Bank reconciliations
Budgets
Correspondence (general)
Employee personnel records (after termination)
Employment applications
Equipment repair records

Insurance policies (expired)
Interim financial reports
Internal audit reports (sometimes these must be keptlonger.)
Internal reports (miscellaneous)
Petty cash vouchers

Seven Years

Accident reports and claims (settled cases)
Accounts payable ledgers and schedules
Accounts receivable ledgers and schedules
Bank statements
Checks (canceled)
Contracts and leases
Correspondence (accounting, credit and collection and
   personnel)
Expense analyses and distribution schedules
Inventories of products, materials and supplies
Invoices from vendors
Invoices to customers
Notes receivable ledgers and schedules
Payroll records and summaries, including payments to
   pensioners
Purchase orders
Sales records (cash and charge)
Scrap and salvage records (inventories, sales, etc.)
Stock and bond certificates (canceled)
Subsidiary ledgers
Time books
Unemployment claims
Voucher register and schedules
Vouchers for payments to vendors, employees, etc. (include
   travel and entertainment allowances and reimbursement)

Permanently

Audit reports of accountants
Canceled checks for important payments, i.e., taxes,
   property purchase, contracts. (Keep with papers for the
   transaction.)

Capital stock and bond records (ledgers, transfer registers, stubs showing issues, interest coupons, options, etc.)

Cash books

Chart of accounts

Charter and by-laws

Contracts and leases still in effect

Correspondence (legal and important matters only)

Deeds, mortgages, title papers and bills of sale

Depreciation schedules

Financial statements (end-of-year)

General and private ledgers (and end-of-year trial balances)

Insurance records, current accident reports, claims, policies

Journals

Minute books of directors' and shareholders' meetings

Patent, trademark and copyright registrations

Property appraisals by outside appraisers

Property records (costs, depreciation reserves and schedules, blueprint and plans)

Tax returns and worksheets, Revenue Agents' Reports and other documents relating to determination of income tax liabilities

■ Appendix C ■

Periodicals, Books and Other Helpful Information Sources

■

Successful entrepreneurs make sure they stay on top of industry trends. They are constantly on the lookout for new information because they understand the importance of being prepared for success. Some of the most helpful information can be found in monthly business magazines.

It is also important to keep developing a general knowledge of business skills. A variety of training materials is available at reasonable costs. Resources that target small businesses are constantly being created. Most of the information that follows can be obtained at your local library or through interlibrary loan. Ask your librarian for assistance.

■ Resources _____

Name of Resource: *Consumer Information Catalog*
Where To Find It: Consumer Information Center-Y
PO Box 100
Pueblo, CO 81002

223

What It Contains: A listing of free and low-cost informational booklets published by various agencies of the Federal Government. Some of the titles specifically for businesses include:

Financial Management: How To Make a Go of Your Business ($2.50)

General Information Concerning Patents (including application) ($2.00)

Reporting and Disclosure Guide for Employee Benefits Plans (Free)

The Small Business Directory (Free) A list of booklets and videos for businesses.

Why Use It: Resource for definitive current information

Name of Resource: *Future Work*
Where To Find It: World Future Society
7910 Woodmont Ave., Ste. 450
Bethesda, MD 20814
(301) 656-8274

Who Could Use It: Anyone—particularly when developing a niche market, marketing plan and/or planning to hire employees

What It Contains: Report by John B. Mahafie of JF Coates, Inc. concerning the work force and business trends in the '90s

Why Use It: To identify key factors in the business/ economic climate that may be most critical to your development—market research

When To Use It: Start-up and growth stages

Name of Resource: *Privileged Information* and *Privileged Breakthrough Information*
Where To Find It: *Boardroom Reports Magazine*
330 W. 42 St.
New York, NY 10036
(800) 234-3834 or (212) 239-9000
Subscription Office
Box 53313 Boulder, CO 80322

What It Contains: A treasure trove of information on all fronts, these publications provide updates on exceptional developments, innovations and developments in taxes, technology, medical and health and other areas of interest to individuals and businesses who need to stay abreast of latest developments.

Why Use It: For latest breaking news in all areas affecting you and your business, this is also an excellent idea resource.

Name of Resource: *Software Review File*
Where To Find It: Local library reference section
Who Could Use It: Any business
What It Contains: This survey of computer software contains an index and a compilation of surveys from leading magazine software review editors.

Name of Resource: *Women in Business Yellow Pages*
Where To Find It: 7358 Lincoln Ave., Ste. 150
Chicago, IL 60646
(312) 679-7800
What It Contains: This directory lists more than 1,000 companies representing a variety of Chicago business products and services. The directory, which has a current circulation of 45,000, also lists special programs, agencies and hotlines offered for women.

Name of Resource: *Your Small Business Survival Guide*
($3 a copy)
Where To Find It: Circulation Department
Nation's Business
1615 H St., N.W.
Washington, DC 20062
(212) 370-1440 or (800) 638-6582
What It Contains: A compilation of the most-asked questions from the editors of "Direct Line," a monthly column in the magazine, *Nation's Business*
When To Use It: Anytime prior to start-up or after

Training and Development

Name of Resource: Barbara Brabec Productions
PO Box 2137
Naperville, IL 60567
Who Could Use It: Home-based businesses, especially those that are craft-oriented.

What It Contains:	Barbara is the author of *Homemade Money* ($21.95 postage paid) and publisher of *National Home Business Report,* published quarterly (sample copy $6). For a free catalog., write to the address listed above.
When To Use It:	Continuous information useful at start-up and after

Name of Resource:	*Business Training Resource Catalog*
Where To Find It:	Department of Commerce and Community Affairs, Illinois Small Business Development Center Network and the Illinois Business Hotline, (800) 252-2923
Who Could Use It:	Anyone in business or planning to go into business
What It Contains:	A publication developed through a partnership between the Illinois Department of Commerce and Community Affairs, the U.S. Small Business Administration and the Small Business Development Center Network as a service to Illinois small businesses. It lists workshops and conferences throughout the Chicago area supported by the U.S. Small Business Administration, and includes advertising, export, financing, government contracts and bidding, insurance, international trade, starting a small business and much more.

Name of Resource:	Dartnell
Where To Find It:	4660 Ravenswood Ave. Chicago IL 60640 (312) 561-4000
What It Contains:	Producers of sales, motivational and management films—write for free film catalog

Name of Resource:	American Institute of Small Business
Where To Find It:	7515 Wayzata Blvd., Ste. 201 Minneapolis, MN 55426 (612) 545-7001
What It Contains:	Comprehensive self-study training materials, books, videos and computer software designed for business start-ups

—*How To Set Up Your Own Small Business* a comprehensive guide designed to walk an individual through all the development stages of a business.

—*Advertising and Public Relations* (Video)

—*How To Write a Marketing Plan* (Video)

When To Use It: Valuable tools for use prior to and during start-up; an invaluable resource for growing businesses

Name of Resource: *Inc. Special Reports*
Where To Find It: PO Box 54129
Boulder, CO 80322
(800) 234-0999
Who Could Use It: Any business, particularly if poised for growth
What It Contains: Numerous business publications and videos

Name of Resource: International Film Bureau
Where To Find It: 332 S. Michigan
Chicago, IL 60604
(312) 427-4545
What It Contains: Educational and industrial films and video cassettes

Name of Resource: *Small Business Training Resource Catalog*
Where To Find It: Illinois Department of Commerce and Community Affairs
Small Business Assistance Bureau
100 W. Randolph, Ste. 3-400
Chicago, IL 60601
(312) 814-3144
What It Contains: A quarterly catalog of activities and training supported by the SBA throughout Illinois

Name of Resource: *Sound Ideas*
Simon & Schuster Audio Cassette Catalog
Where To Find It: PO Box 11071
Des Moines, IA 50336
(515) 284-6751
What It Contains: A wide selection of audio cassettes designed to educate and enhance your business skills, sharpen your communications

skills, help you achieve success and become an effective manager, enhance your selling power, motivate you and earn you more money.

Name of Resource:	*Successful Business Management*
Where To Find It:	Published by The Hume Group
	835 Franklin Ct.
	Marietta, GA 30067
	(800) 222-4863
What It Contains:	This self-study course covers money management, business planning, marketing, managing people, law, insurance and tax strategies and much more for the small business person.

Name of Resource:	U.S. Savings Bond Division—Film Library
Where To Find It:	U.S. Treasury Dept.
	Washington, DC 20226
	(202) 622-2000
Who Could Use It:	Anyone
What It Contains:	Information is provided concerning money matters applicable to the small business in videos such as *Advantages and Ways of Purchasing Bonds Through Payroll Savings Plans*, etc.

———————————————————— ∎

Periodicals

Take a trip to your public library or bookstore when you have some extra time, and examine several of the magazines listed below. Start by just leafing through the table of contents. Try to hold off reading an article until you have gone through at least ten magazines. Jot down the pages and dates of the magazines that interest you. This is the best way to get a good impression of the type of articles each magazine prints. Look for special columns that might be of interest to your business. Several of the major small business publications currently available include:

■ Resources

Name of Resource:	*About Women's Business*
Where To Find It:	Chicago Institute for Economic Development and Women's Business Development Center
	Women's Business Development Center
	8 S. Michigan, Ste. 400
	Chicago, IL 60603
	(312) 853-3477
What It Contains:	A quarterly publication committed to women's economic self-sufficiency through business ownership, this is an excellent resource for helping women business owners identify and locate support networks and resources.

Name of Resource:	*Black Enterprise*
Where To Find It:	Subscription Service Center
	PO Box 3011
	Harlan, IA 51593-2102
	(800) 727-7777
What It Contains:	This magazine, which focuses on African-American issues in small business, features excellent articles and resources that any entrepreneur could use.

Name of Resource:	*Business Ethics*
Where To Find It:	1107 Hazeltine Blvd., Ste. 530
	Chaska, MN 55318
	(612) 448-8864
What It Contains:	The mission of this relatively new magazine is to promote ethical business practices, to serve the growing community of professionals (and business owners) striving to live and work in responsible ways and to create financially healthy companies in the process. *Business Ethics* contains motivating action-producing articles on opportunities to give back to our communities while prospering individually.

Name of Resource:	*Entrepreneur*
Where To Find It:	PO Box 1987
	Irvine, CA 92713-9787
	(800) 421-2300
What It Contains:	Mostly geared toward service start-ups, this magazine offers a number of "how-to" guides for starting a wide variety of businesses, including a gift basket service, wedding planning, and auto detailing. Also included are guides for writing your business plan, promoting your business and even getting into seminar development, a good source of additional revenues for many service-based companies. Relatively inexpensive, practical advice is provided to eliminate the common pitfalls of starting and building a successful business.

Name of Resource:	*Entrepreneurial Woman*
Where To Find It:	Subscription Department
	PO Box 53792
	Boulder, CO 80321-3792
	(800) 284-5534
What It Contains:	What we like in particular about this magazine is its down-to-earth approach to starting and growing a business. *Entrepreneurial Woman* offers many special pieces of information for women-owned businesses.

Name of Resource:	*Harvard Business Review*
Where To Find It:	Subscriber Service
	PO Box 52623
	Boulder, CO 80322-2623
	(800) 274-3214
What It Contains:	*Harvard Business Review* offers seasoned entrepreneurs and business managers in-depth articles and reports concerning issues and trends of interest to growth-positioned businesses.

Name of Resource: *Home Office Computing*
Where To Find It: Home Office Computing
PO Box 51344
Boulder, CO 80321-1344
(800) 678-0118

What It Contains: A monthly magazine filled with information on all facets of businesses—marketing, management, finance and, of course, computing. The magazine helps you automate your business, and helps you stay abreast of current developments in home business technology and computerization.

Name of Resource: *Illinois Small Business Bulletin*
Where To Find It: Department of Commerce and Community Affairs
100 W. Randolph, Ste. 3-400
Chicago, IL 60601
or call:
Illinois Business Hotline (800) 252-2923

What It Contains: A publication of the Illinois Department of Commerce & Community Affairs, the *Bulletin* offers up-to-date information about key small business issues and activities.

Name of Resource: *Inc. Magazine*
Where To Find It: INC Publishing Corp.
PO Box 54129
Boulder, CO 80322
(800) 234-0999

What It Contains: A monthly business magazine for growing companies (up to $100 million in sales) and CEOs, *Inc.* publishes the INC 500—the top 500 small businesses in the United States on a yearly basis. A resource section is included for business owners to ask questions and receive answers in subsequent issues from fellow readers and resource experts.

Name of Resource: *Kiplinger's Personal Finance Magazine*
Where To Find It: Editors Park, MD 20782
(800) 544-0155

What It Contains: One of the better monthly magazines dedicated to the evaluation and reporting of current economic trends. Annually updated booklets on new tax revisions and consequences are available.

Name of Resource: *The Kiplinger Tax Letter*
Where To Find It: 1729 H St., N.W.
Washington, DC 20006
(800) 544-0155

What It Contains: *The Tax Letter* offers up-to-date information concerning taxes, current tax laws and new bills, while providing increased insight that will enable you to make intelligent tax-planning decisions now.

Name of Resource: *The Kiplinger Washington Letter*
Where To Find It: The Kiplinger Washington Editors
1729 H St., N.W.
Washington, DC 20006-3938
(800) 544-0155

What It Contains: This weekly newsletter offers timely information concerning business and economic trends and developments that will help you stay abreast of national developments

Name of Resource: *Minority Business Entrepreneur*
Where To Find It: 924 N. Market St.
Inglewood, CA 90302
(213) 673-9398 FAX: (213) 673-0170

What It Contains: A very fine publication that informs minority and women-owned businesses about business opportunities. Articles run the gamut from contract procurement, to case studies on model companies, to more general topics such as bringing quality into the work place. Among other benefits, this magazine offers opportunities for locating new customers.

Name of Resource: *Nation's Business*
Where To Find It: Subscription Department
PO Box 51062
Boulder, CO 80321-1062
(212) 370-1440 or (800) 638-6582
What It Contains: Published by the United States Chamber of Commerce, this publication offers practical advice for the small business owner. Special sections include "Direct Line," which offers informational resources for answers to marketing, finance and management questions.

Name of Resource: *Success*
Where To Find It: PO Box 3036
Harlan, IA 51593-2097
(800) 234-7324
What It Contains: Called "the magazine for today's entrepreneurial mind," this magazine connotes the truest form of entrepreneurism. Started back in 1891, *Success* recognized the pioneering spirit of the successful small business owner. One hundred years later, the magazine continues to showcase successful entrepreneurs as well as those aspiring start-ups. Special yearly features include a *Success Gold 100*, a cooperative effort with Arthur Andersen & Co. ranking the most solid and promising opportunities in franchising (around November of each year), and an annual *Money Issue* that provides several pages on raising money (around December of each year). Great feature stories and excellent book and software reviews are offered monthly. Most issues have a central theme of strong interest to entrepreneurs.

Name of Resource: *Working Woman*
Where To Find It: Hal Publications, Inc.
342 Madison Ave.
New York, NY 10173
(212) 309-9800

What It Contains: A wonderful monthly magazine for executive, professional and entrepreneurial women, median age 34. The material, focused on work-related issues, is sophisticated (not entry-level) and witty.

Radio Talk Show—Business Advice

Name of Resource: "Business Opportunities" 12 noon Saturdays (1 hour), "Your Own Success" 1:00 P.M. Saturdays (1 hour) and "Women's Business Exchange" 1:00 P.M. Sunday

Where To Find It: WNVR-AM (1030)

What It Contains: Information and advice specifically directed to the small business person/entrepreneur

Why Use It: For updated information

Name of Resource: Business Radio Network (BRN)

Where To Find It: 888 Garden of the Gods Road
Colorado Springs, CO 80907
(719) 528-7040 or (800) 321-2349

What It Contains: Call or write BRN for a list of nationally syndicated business radio shows in your area, including Paul and Sarah Edward's "Home Office Show," "Women's Business Exchange," "SCAMs America," "The New Venture Money Show" (a support forum for start-ups), and "Grand Opening," (on the franchise industry).

Their local affiliate, WNVR (1030 AM) Chicago, carries: "Home Office Show," every Sunday night on Business Radio Network. The show provides five minutes of helpful advice on technological and business issues for people in home offices by *Home Office Computing* editor-in-chief, Claudia Cohl. The hour-long show airs at 10:00 P.M. EST (9:00 P.M. CST).

Let Us Hear From You

Entrepreneurial Resources

Listed below are my recommendations for resources that have been especially helpful to the development of my business:

Name of Resource:

Where To Find It:

What It Contains:

Why Use It:

When To Use It:

Name of Resource:

Where To Find It:

What It Contains:

Why Use It:

When To Use It:

Please Send To: Melissa Giovagnoli
The HAIMS Group
1901 N. Roselle Rd., Ste. 500
Schaumburg, IL 60195

■ Index ■